Manufacturers, Mummies and Manchester

Two hundred years of interest in and study of Egyptology in the Greater Manchester area

Hilary Forrest

BAR British Series 532
2011

Published in 2016 by
BAR Publishing, Oxford

BAR British Series 532

Manufacturers, Mummies and Manchester

ISBN 978 1 4073 0788 6

BAR Publishing is the trading name of British Archaeological Reports (Oxford) Ltd.
British Archaeological Reports was first incorporated in 1974 to publish the BAR
Series, International and British. In 1992 Hadrian Books Ltd became part of the BAR
group. This volume was originally published by Archaeopress in conjunction with
British Archaeological Reports (Oxford) Ltd / Hadrian Books Ltd, the Series principal
publisher, in 2011. This present volume is published by BAR Publishing, 2016.

Printed in England

BAR
PUBLISHING

BAR titles are available from:

BAR Publishing
122 Banbury Rd, Oxford, OX2 7BP, UK
EMAIL info@barpublishing.com
PHONE +44 (0)1865 310431
FAX +44 (0)1865 316916
www.barpublishing.com

Contents

Acknowledgements

Those who have helped to bring this book into the light of day are too numerous to mention individually. I should like to thank all those people who have given their time and shared their knowledge with me so generously. Throughout my research I have received unfailingly courteous help and encouragement, whether from professional bodies, academics or personal contacts.

There are two people without whom this book would not have been written. Particular thanks are due to my fellow Egyptophile, Hilary Kelly, who has been a stalwart supporter and an indispensible practical helper. She has given hours of her time as my 'shabti', always standing by, like the servants of the Egyptian afterlife, saying 'here I am, I shall do it'. I could not have completed the task without her invaluable help in the preparation of this manuscript.

The other person I should like to thank is Professor Rosalie David whose positive encouragement and practical help in providing contacts and smoothing the path of my research have been inspirational. The second half of the book is offered as a tribute to her work and achievements.

Preface

When the ancient Egyptians buried their dead, with elaborate rituals and funerary practices, they were hoping to achieve eternal life. The deceased individual became the Osiris, the personification of the god who presided over the underworld. What they left behind became the focus, first for robbers, then for collectors and finally for scholars. The first two, in their blind rush for the most valuable or outstanding examples of material they could find, showed scant respect for the people whose tombs they were violating. The scholars had more insight into the real lives of those who had been buried with such care.

In recent times there has been a debate about whether human remains should be on display in museums, and, by implication, whether they should be the subject of study. Those who feel that they should not, may not realise that by respectful study and careful reconstruction of aspects of ancient life and culture, the scientists are giving their subjects exactly what they craved, a form of immortality. The unnamed mummy numbered 1770, for example, unwrapped with great care in Manchester Museum in 1975, belonged to a young girl whose name may have been forgotten, but whose life and even whose appearance, have been given a new meaning.

When I was a child, being brought up in the Home Counties, my Mancunian father always maintained that his native city was the cultural centre of Britain. It had the best, the biggest, the first, of everything and always thought today what the world would think tomorrow. He believed, like many of his compatriots, that Manchester was ahead of the game in industry, economic prosperity and achievement. This was indeed how the city must have seemed to a boy brought up in Edwardian England; 'Cottonopolis' was at its peak. The city centre was full of top-hatted businessmen on their way to deal in cotton at the Royal Exchange. The new Ship Canal connected the manufacturing and trading areas directly to the sea and the potential seemed unlimited.

The prosperity enjoyed by the city of Manchester was shared by the neighbouring cotton manufacturing towns. Many of these have now, in some cases unwillingly, become part of the Greater Manchester conurbation, although it seems doubtful whether many of the textile magnates of Bolton, Rochdale and Ashton, for example, would have been impressed by the idea of being part of a greater whole. The centres of these towns reflect the wealth and the great sense of civic pride which prevailed throughout much of the nineteenth and well into the twentieth century.

All these towns were centres of great wealth at the end of the nineteenth century and the magnates who had amassed personal fortunes were frequently people of high ideals, based on their liberal and non-conformist views, who were keen to use their wealth to benefit others. As one of the major sources of high quality cotton was Egypt, links were forged between the two centres. For this reason, one of the industrialists' chosen methods of benefitting their communities was to invest funds in Egyptian excavations. In return, they, or their towns, received a share of the finds which could then be put on display for the education and edification of the people. This meant that some of the most important collections of Egyptian material are in the North West of England, in Manchester itself and in the textile towns surrounding it. These great collections are a unique resource and have allowed the development of pioneering work.

This book traces interest in Egyptology in Manchester and the surrounding towns from the early nineteenth century, when interest in Egypt first developed, through travel and business links, to the benefactions and dedicated work of cotton men and women who helped to build up and to display the remarkable collections which can be seen to this day.

The second half of the book starts in the middle of the twentieth century when the focus became more scientific. The Manchester Mummy Project was pioneering in its day and the Manchester Protocol which laid down a tested methodology for mummy studies became accepted world-wide. Since its inception, mummy studies in Manchester have gone from strength to strength and the KNH Centre for Biomedical Egyptology is now pursuing ground-breaking research. At the same time, a substantial number of local people, drawn from all walks of life, have become deeply involved in Egyptology through the educational opportunities which the area has offered. Some of these have themselves become professionals in the field, providing access to the subject for yet more enthusiasts. Though it is impossible to mention everyone involved, the last section explores a selection of notable contributors to the Egyptological scene in Manchester.

List of illustrations

Part 1

The Establishment of Egyptology in Manchester

1. Travellers and Collectors

Plundering from the ancient Egyptians has a long and ignoble history stretching back into antiquity. Although tomb robbers over the millennia had already removed most of the material which had been buried with their ancestors, the tradition of taking from tombs and monuments was not restricted to antiquity. The use of mummies in medical treatments was common from the Middle Ages onwards and a brisk trade developed. As the western world opened up to travel after the Renaissance, a keen interest in other Egyptian items was born. These were recognised more as curiosities than as works of art, since the culture from which they came was a completely closed book. The passion for collecting became fashionable in the seventeenth century as travel became an essential part of a western European gentleman's education and, of course, the collection of souvenirs became de rigueur. Some visitors to Egypt took a scholarly approach, recognising the need to study antiquities in a quasi-scientific manner. In the reign of Louis XIV for example, some of his subjects, while in Egypt to acquire antiquities for the royal collection, carried out a large number of explorations, especially in the Great Pyramid. [1] During these expeditions many hieroglyphic inscriptions were copied, thus combining acquisitiveness with serious study. The activities of these travellers and many others began a tradition which gained a new focus with the Napoleonic invasion of Egypt in 1798. A Scientific and Artistic Commission was set up to survey Egypt, in order to facilitate Napoleon's colonisation process. Their work was published in the huge, nineteen volume 'Description de l'Egypte' between 1809 and 1828.

Many collections of Egyptian material already existed outside Egypt and the depredations of unscrupulous collectors had already caused much damage before the Napoleonic record could be made. By 1805 Mohammed Ali, the Pasha of Egypt, had realised the importance to Egypt of its past and had for the first time set up regulations about the excavation and export of artefacts. This should, in theory, have restricted such activities. Instead it tended to force them underground. The material which rested in both public and private collections was still a mystery since the inscriptions, which could provide the key to its significance, were not yet deciphered. There were scholars who had advanced theories about their meaning, as far back as the ancient Greeks, but most of these ideas were mistaken. The final breakthrough came through the work of Thomas Young, and, more famously Jean Francois Champollion in the early 1820s and it changed the whole perception of ancient Egypt. The rush to enhance collections outside Egypt gained momentum once the key had been found. Exploits of men like Belzoni

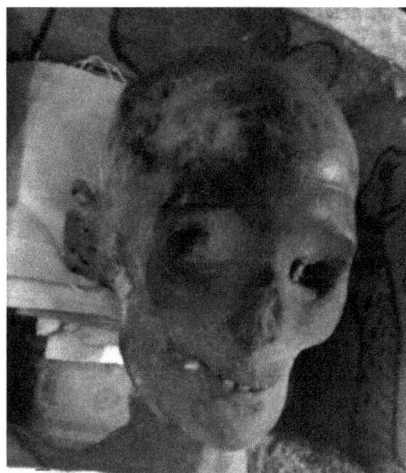

Fig.1 Asru

and the patronage of foreign diplomats such as Henry Salt and Bernadino Drovetti helped to lay the foundation of the great European Egyptian museum collections, such as those in London and Turin. The transport of the colossal head of Ramesses II from the Ramesseum to the British Museum by the former circus strongman Belzoni, is legendary.

As the nineteenth century progressed, the creation of private collections of varying sizes, not only in London, but in the provinces too, attracted the interest of wealthy patrons. In the north of England, the development of industry had created fortunes for the owners who had large disposable incomes. In the area around and near to Manchester, textiles, mainly cotton and related industries, were the most important sources of wealth. Egyptian antiquities were of particular interest to these wealthy collectors for a number of reasons, which included a religious element as well as business involvement in Egyptian cotton production. As early as 1819, a Manchester traveller, John Hyde, ventured as far as the first cataract on the Nile and kept a journal. In common with many other travellers, Hyde heedlessly carved his name at Abusir.[2]

In 1825 the first of many mummies is recorded as having appeared in Manchester. It was a gift to the Manchester Natural History Society Museum from William and Robert Garnett. According to Fildes, they may have been the ancestors of the Garnett family who ran Trotters and Garnett, a shop near the medical school, which sold medical instruments. There is no way of knowing how long it had been in England.[3] It was that of Asru, a chantress of Amun. It was possibly found in Thebes but there was no

[1] David, Rosalie, 1993 pp. 18-20

[2] Bierbrier, M.J., 1995 edition p. 213
[3] Fildes, George, 1970s

provenance with the two coffins and the mummy, which had been unwrapped at an earlier date.

Later, after the foundation of the Manchester Museum in the University, Asru was to have a prominent position in the Egyptian collection. She became a central focus of the Manchester Mummy project in the 1970s when her remains, which included a package of mummified viscera, were subjected to modern scientific scrutiny and she still fascinates modern visitors to the museum.

Still later in the nineteenth century, Manchester was to be the recipient of a major collection of Egyptian antiquities through the generosity of a cotton magnate, Jesse Haworth, who was part of a social circle in the area which had a strong religious inclination as well as a keen intellectual curiosity about Egypt.

Long before Haworth's involvement, one traveller, a Bolton textile producer, Mr Heywood, left two revealing accounts of his visit to Egypt in 1845. They provide an insight into some of the western attitudes to contemporary Egyptian culture, as well as a view on the antiquities visited.[4] One of these documents is a letter in which he describes Alexandria and its inhabitants. He mentions Pompey's pillar, and gives a description of what he saw which included egrets, water buffalo and wild boar. In a talk he gave, once back in Bolton,[5] he provided a more detailed description of Alexandria revealing an interest in history. The writer's more particular fascination however, is shown by references to watching the loading of cotton in many places and noting that it came by camel. During their passage to Cairo he notes 'In the course of our passage we met numerous boats loaden (sic) with cotton on their way to Alexandria'. Later in the nineteenth century and well into the twentieth, Alexandria was to be a major supplier of cotton to Manchester. The Royal Exchange in the city has preserved the boards which show its last day of trading in 1969 and the name Alexandria appears on it.

Heywood and his companion found the heat in Cairo too much and had to keep washing in cold water. He appears to have been disappointed in the city, remarking rather sourly that there was 'Too much oil in some of the dishes and too little upon the axles of some of the public vehicles...to be agreeable either to the palate or the ear, or, (referring to the donkeys pulling the carts) of the ear of the poor animal.'

As most western tourists of the period did, they climbed the pyramid, though not without some assistance, and then went inside after a breakfast of eggs, fowl, tongue and sherbet. A French companion, in a typical tourist act, oblivious to any possible consequences or effects on the interior, fired his gun in the Great Pyramid to get the 'extraordinary reverberations'. Heywood tells us that the Sphinx 'is said to be done in honour of the ancient Kings of Egypt'. Whilst in Cairo, they visited a slave market and Heywood notes with disapproval that they were offered

a young Nubian slave for £20. He shows some concern for the welfare of ordinary Egyptians when he visits the palace of the Pasha, Mahomet. The palace may have been grand but he comments that 'the people (are) ill governed and not receiving a fair reward for their labour' a point which he develops. His talk concludes with a wish that 'those who have visited this singular country must wish that they should not only have straw for their bricks but that their general condition should be greatly ameliorated and that they long be distinguished as an ancient and a happy country'.

The visit to the palace had been arranged by a local contact. 'I and my friend were more formally introduced as two English travellers as had been agreed upon'. Presumably there was some attempt at a subtle approach with a view, perhaps, of acquiring business. The Pasha, who was described as a venerable old man with a long white beard, gave them coffee.

'I stated through an interpreter that I was engaged in the cotton manufacture. He immediately asked if I used the Egyptian cotton to which I replied in the affirmative, but at the same time informed him that I was not a spinner but used it in the manufacture of fine thread used in quilting for vests. I also mentioned my interest in bleaching and finishing.' Heywood seems to have complimented the quality of the Egyptian product but he continues, 'I went on to state, which had been suggested by one of our friends before leaving England that it required better cleaning. Perceiving this remark not to be well received, I added that I believed it had recently undergone some improvement.' Heywood retrieved his tactlessness by promising as they left 'to make some return by shewing his agents our manufactory whenever they happened to visit our country.' Although there is no evidence that Heywood kept his promise, he was foreshadowing the future strong links, which were to develop later in the century between the thriving cotton industry in Bolton and the producers of fine Egyptian cotton.

It was not only businessmen who visited Egypt. Some went purely for cultural reasons, although even such pure motives did not preclude the acquisition of ancient artefacts on the way. John Gadsby, the son of a Baptist Minister in Manchester travelled extensively in the Middle East, collecting items, which he sold on to the British Museum. He became a publisher in Manchester and London and produced a two-volume account of his travels, entitled 'My Wanderings in the East'.[6]

As the nineteenth century progressed, whilst more and more visits with scholarly goals were carried out and more businessmen, particularly those involved in textiles visited Egypt to enhance their trade, interest in travel of the kind which would now be called 'tourism' was also developing rapidly. Visitors might be in groups organised by Mr. Thomas Cook, or they might be independent travellers of considerable means. The latter were inclined to look down

---

[4] Heywood, R.Undated
[5] Heywood, R.1845

[6] Bierbrier, M.J., 1995 edition p. 159

TRAVELLERS AND COLLECTORS

Fig. 2 Marianne Brocklehurst

Fig.3 Sketch by Marianne Brocklehurst

scientific ends in view; and the usual surplus of idlers who travel for the mere love of travel or the satisfaction of a purposeless curiosity'. One imagines that the tourist groups would certainly come under the heading of 'satisfaction of a purposeless curiosity'[7] in Miss Edwards' eyes.

Some travellers combined several of these desires. A typical example of this was Marianne Brocklehurst who was born and bred in the Macclesfield area, not far from Manchester.

Like many who became involved in Egyptology in North West England, she had a connection with textiles. Unlike those further to the north, whose interest was in cotton, she came from a Unitarian family whose fortune was largely based on silk, for which Macclesfield was famous. She had a lifelong interest in travel and was a photographer of professional standard. She and her close friend Mary Booth travelled the Nile in 1873, looking for subjects to draw and to photograph, collecting artefacts which included a mummy, and generally satisfying a great love of travel. Her diary provides a lively and illuminating insight into what tourism was like in those days. They hired a dahabeeyah or Nile sailing boat which they immediately named 'Bagstones' after their own house in Cheshire, thus establishing a homely link. Miss Brocklehurst's illustrations for her journal show the two ladies respectably, and one might think, suffocatingly, clad in long, full skirts and solar topees with neck veils to keep off the sun.[8]

on the organised groups. Amelia Edwards who became the prime mover in setting up the Egypt Exploration Fund was a professional writer, mainly of popular novels, who travelled to Egypt in 1873. Her perspicacious summary of her fellow-travellers describes 'invalids in search of health, artists in search of subjects, sportsmen keen on crocodiles; special correspondents alert for gossip; collectors on the scent of papyri and mummies; men of science with only

---

[7] A.B. Edwards,1877 p. 3
[8] Miss Brocklehurst on the Nile, 2004 p. 90

Fig. 4 Marianne Brocklehurst and nephew Alfred

Fig. 5 Miss Brocklehurst disturbed by the locals

As it happened, the two companions, early on in their visit, met Amelia Edwards and her friend Lucy Renshawe, who were also sailing the Nile in a dahabeeyah named the 'Philae'. They became not only friends, but also rivals for the acquisition of ancient objects. In her biography of Amelia Edwards, Joan Rees, explains that, 'the friendship which developed offered welcome companionship and also a spice of friendly, though fierce, rivalry at times....The ladies of each boat bargained heartily for antiques.[9] Miss Brocklehurst eventually amassed a considerable collection which included a fine jewelled collar which Miss Edwards described in her book. She felt it might have been worn by an Egyptian Princess.[10]

An appendix to Miss Brocklehurst's diary is called 'How we got our mummy'. It illustrates vividly some of the less scrupulous methods engaged in by travellers of the period, who undoubtedly considered them fair in the game of antiquity collection and who had no qualms about outwitting 'the natives'. While visiting Thebes, the 'MBs', as she referred to herself and her companion, encountered an artist friend whom they had met earlier on the journey. He took them to visit an Arab family who lived in a rock-cut tomb with many chambers. They were entertained according to the laws of Arab hospitality, though she confesses to having poured away her 'coffee of a horrid description' in a dark corner where it refused to soak into the ground, running embarrassingly across the floor in front of her hosts. They were taken deeper into the bowels of the tomb where 'we were hoisted perhaps twelve or fifteen feet high by the strong arms of our black friends' up a kind of chimney. Here they found their mummy 'in its very prettily painted case (white ground and coloured figures) and all enclosed in a wooden sarcophagus more than an inch in thickness, which from its size and weight was necessarily out of all question from a smuggling point of view'. She goes on to remark that the mummy could have been no-one of importance since there was no gold on the coffin. 'We liked its looks however and we liked the idea of smuggling on a large scale under the nose of the Pasha's guards who, as excavations were going on nearby, were pretty thick on the ground and on the alert.'

The tone of this account is very revealing. The 'M Bs' were clearly excited by the thrill of the chase in much the same way as nephew Alfred, their travelling companion, who seems to have spent all his time in Egypt blasting small birds out of the sky – large ones too, and even crocodiles came into his sights. There seems to be no whisper of guilt attached to the smuggling of this contraband which, after some hitches, was pushed through a window of the dahabeeyah and then hidden in a closet. The operation took more than one attempt; the ladies being somewhat perturbed in case the smugglers had been arrested. They were relieved to find that the mummy had been taken to the house of a friend 'the same house from which we had smuggled the papyrus away in the sleeve of a thick Inverness coat the night previous'.

The author then makes a rather barbed and revealing comment about the local population, which sheds an interesting light on European attitudes of the period. She says it was 'a very hot night too and if the Arabs had brains, which they haven't, it might have struck someone as an odd thing to wear on such occasion'.

Although the ladies did not know it at the time, Amelia Edwards was also trying to acquire the same mummy and papyrus. In 'A thousand miles up the Nile' there seems to be a whiff of sour grapes on the part of the unsuccessful bidder, for she remarks that the 'MBs' had 'bought the mummy and the papyrus at an enormous price; and then, unable to endure the perfume of their ancient Egyptian, drowned the dear departed at the end of the week.'[11] The perfume does appear to have caused a problem, though Marianne's account of what happened subsequently is somewhat at odds with that of Miss Edwards. The biggest worry does appear to have been the 'suspicious odour in the passage near the closet where the Mummy was concealed and we feared lest the cook in particular who had been in the service of Mariette Bey himself and doubtless was

---

[9] Rees, Joan 1998 p. 39
[10] Edwards, Amelia B 1877 p. 350

[11] Edwards, Amelia B 1877 p. 660

acquainted with the peculiar mummy 'bouquet' might sniff him out and bring us all to grief.' She acknowledges that Mariette Bey was said to be very 'stern and cruel with these contrabandists if he catches them' though she goes on to point out that 'it is whispered that in the capacity of Conservator of the Antiquities of Egypt, he manages to do a little that way on his own account, and that not a few little things find themselves in the Paris museum instead of that of Boulaq.'

Once the mummy was safely on board it was declared to be 'altogether a festive object and not at all a funereal frump'. Later, the coffin was sawn open and the occupant revealed. Miss Booth has bought a small saw, especially for the purpose. The examination of the mummy was hardly a scientific exercise, since the main purpose seems to have been to look for ornaments, scarabs and even a 'little god or two' in amongst the bandages. Alas for the hopeful collectors their mummy was 'a little boy, about twelve years old' with no such treasures in his bandages. They carefully re-wrapped the bandages round him and buried him by night with great secrecy and left him in his native land. The mummy had dry, hard and shiny skin 'like good old oak' and 'the features of his face were really pleasant and happy in expression and there was hair on his woodeny little head'. Much later, back in England, it was discovered from the hieroglyphs, to have been a female body.

The mummy had been buried, but the challenge now was to smuggle its case out of Egypt. 'We devoutly hoped it might escape the prying fingers of the dreaded police who were waiting for us at Cairo, at Alexandria, everywhere'. The cases with their antiquities passed without search but a second batch of luggage, containing no contraband was thoroughly scrutinised. The antiquities were safely 'bribed on board the steamer'. There is perhaps a trace of smugness in the author's final comment that they had been lucky 'whilst others were not' as 'in the case of our friends on the Philae, who had all their antiquities seized at Alexandria and are doubtful if they will ever be able to recover them'.[12] No wonder Miss Edwards was a little bitter.

Marianne's record of her visits to Egypt took the form of a sketch book as well as her journal. Her pen and ink and watercolour pictures give a vivid impression of the country and its people. Two particularly remarkable and historically valuable ones show the removal of the priestly mummies from the cache at Deir el Bahri in 1891. She happened to be in the vicinity when this event took place and felt compelled to record it.

The two sketches show the removal of the coffins, some of the local population, and a small group of interested observers including the 'MBs.' The first is captioned 'Winding up the mummy cases and mummies of priests and priestesses of Amon (XXIst dynasty) found hidden in a vault 40 feet below the surface near Der ei Bahari

Fig. 6 The Ramesseum by M. Brocklehurst

Fig. 7 Interior of West Park museum c.1899

in1891. M. Bouriant superintending'. The people shown are named as M.B., Alice Booth (Mary Booth's sister), Mary Musters, Achmed Effendi, M.I. Booth, M. Bouriant, on the left, their donkeys, and nearby Canon Taylor with his wife and daughter. The second sketch shows 'Arabs carrying the mummies to the Nile for transportation by dahabeeiahs to Cairo'

Marianne Brocklehurst and her friend travelled far and wide over the next years, collecting knowledge and artefacts and her collection was provided with its own museum at West Park in Macclesfield where the famous mummy case can be seen together with a wide assortment of objects, including scarabs, shabtis, canopic jars and stelae which were catalogued by Rosalie David in 1980.[13] The collection also contains Marianne's sketch books and note-books which reveal her talent as a water-colourist. Sadly, Marianne did not live to see the opening, dying just a few weeks before it.

The ladylike rivalries between Miss Brocklehurst and Miss Edwards were as nothing compared with those of some of the men of the period. The Reverend Greville Chester, who spent a good deal of time in Egypt for the sake of his health,

[12] Miss Brocklehurst on the Nile, 2004 p. 116

[13] David, A.R 1980.

occupied himself in acquiring artefacts on behalf of English collectors. He knew many of those involved in Egyptology in the late nineteenth century including the most notable excavator, William Flinders Petrie. Chester's letters to Petrie reveal some of his attitudes and, more interestingly, his activities. In one of them he makes adverse comments on the Egyptian authorities' policy of granting firmans or permits to local diggers rather than Petrie himself. A letter of March 11th 1887 says 'it is monstrous that an English gentleman who is working scientifically and gently should not have the same 'privilege' as any Arab fellah who chooses to apply for leave to dig'.[14]

Most of the other surviving letters describe his acquisition of a wide variety of artefacts. He apparently rivalled Wallis Budge of the British Museum, (of whom both he and Petrie seem to have had a low opinion) and he became involved in bidding wars to beat 'The Pasha'. He remarks, with great glee that, 'poor Budge went cursing and swearing about Cairo denouncing friends and enemies alike – even his host General Grenfell, and he accused me of keeping back the best things from the B.M!' Poor Budge was known as 'the Bugbear' in Petrie's correspondence and it may be that Budge's humble origins had some influence here, since he had been born to a single mother and was thus 'not quite a gentleman'. A letter from Amelia Edwards to Petrie dated October 1886[15] mentions Budge in a rather critical tone. She suggests that Budge has acquired a gold handle, which should have been sent to Boston. In compensation she suggests that a list of alternative items should be sent there. The implication seems to be that Budge was not always scrupulous in his actions.

One of the items acquired by Chester and supplied by him to a Manchester businessman, Mr. Jesse Haworth, was exhibited in 1887 at the Manchester Jubilee Exhibition. It was Haworth's wish that this treasure should be made available for public view. It was described in the catalogue as the 'throne-chair of Hatasoo'. It was placed under the dome of the Jubilee Exhibition, together with what Jesse Haworth, speaking to the Manchester Egyptian and Oriental Society many years later, in 1912,[16] described as a chess board and a set of chess. By 1912 'Hatasoo' was known by the more familiar name of Hatshepsut and the 'chess set' would nowadays be identified as the Egyptian game of *Senet*. In a letter of 1890, Chester describes how he exported these items from Egypt under the Greek consular seal, in order to outwit the Egyptian authorities who would have been unwilling to interfere with diplomatic packages.

In his autobiography Petrie comments 'I never used such surreptitious help myself, as all I found was pledged to be shown to the Department under whose permit I worked and the bought things were always passed by Maspero, unless so important that he required them'.[17] Maspero

was at that time the head of the Antiquities Department in Cairo and responsible for issuing permits to dig, so Petrie was wise to stay within the agreement. Chester's rather unscrupulous approach is further demonstrated in a letter to Petrie in 1887 in which Chester refers to a location he has indicated 'on the left hand side, just within the second division of the corridor of the tomb of Rameses IX. I think there is a sort of niche over the place'. He continues 'as the purchaser of the throne is the provider of the money you have to work with I think this ought to be done, but you must not let out the reason why you dig in that particular place to anyone'. It seems more than likely that this refers to the throne of Hatshepsut and that the 'purchaser' is Jesse Haworth. In a letter to Petrie on January 21st 1890, Chester refers to the acquisition of more artefacts 'Oh, I have got 3 more bits of carved wood and a small ivory box from the site of the Haworth throne, which has not been cleaned out. Between ourselves an ivory inlaid camp stool was found also, a fine thing but far inferior to the Throne.'

Amelia Edwards herself took a personal interest in the transport and display of these items at the Jubilee Exhibition. She already had a number of contacts in the Manchester area with whom she carried on a regular correspondence. A scribbled note on the corner of a letter to one of her correspondents, Aquila Dodgson, who lived in Ashton under Lyne, says 'throne coming by troop-ship by the kind offices of Sir N. Grenfell'. She hoped to come to Manchester to see the display for herself but was prevented by health considerations from doing so. Instead she suggested to Aquila Dodgson that she proposed to visit Manchester in the autumn 'when I shall have returned from our annual three months at Weston-super-Mare…I could come with a calm mind.' After all, as she pointed out 'the throne has waited for so many centuries as far as I am concerned that I suppose it will hold together for a few months longer and my kind Manchester friends will be less occupied and less overdone with frantic calls and private hospitality when the exhibition excitement has abated.' Later in the same month Amelia wrote to Mr. Dodgson about the display of the throne, agreeing that Mrs. Haworth's idea of draping a leopard skin over it was far better than anything she herself could think of. A few days later she mentions the 'chessmen' wich she says are really 'draughtsmen' that Mr. Chester is selling, together with two slate palettes. 'I'm certain Mr. Haworth would not want to lose them so you may as well include them.' He (presumably Chester) gave either £50 or £60 the lot.' According to Miss Edwards, Mr. Chester intended the whole lot to go to the British Museum but Mr. Birch, the keeper, refused them. The throne was given to the Nation when the Jubilee Exhibition finished. The authorities of the British Museum pledged themselves to give the throne a good and central position for permanent exhibition.[18] The engraving of it below can be found in Amelia Edwards' 'Pharaohs, Fellahs and Explorers'.[19]

[14] Greville Chester to WMF Petrie 1884-1892
[15] Letter from Amelia Edwards to WFM Petrie, Oct.19th, 1886. Petrie Museum
[16] Report of the Manchester Egyptian and Oriental Society 1912
[17] Petrie ,W.M. Flinders 1931 p. 22

[18].Edwards, Amelia B.1892
[19] Manchester Examiner, 1894

Fig. 8 The 'throne'

Subsequently a further piece of wood was discovered, leading to its identification as a bed rather than a throne and, though no longer on display, it remains in the museum to this day. In a lecture given by Miss Edwards, she speculates that the exotic nature of the woods from which it is constructed may mean that they were part of the haul brought back from Hatshepsut's famous expedition to Punt.[20]

Not all the material from Egypt which arrived in Manchester in the late nineteenth century was initially destined for the Haworth collection. In December 1893, the mummy of an adult male named Khary, together with his body coffin, was brought to England. They were eventually donated to the Manchester Museum in 1935 by Lt. Colonel Magnus of Cheadle, Cheshire. The mummy, of uncertain provenance, had been partly unwrapped before it arrived at the museum, though the body coffin is well preserved.

This mummy was recorded by the press as the oldest passenger to be transported on the Manchester Ship Canal. This engineering triumph was the area's pride and joy at the time, having only recently been opened, enhancing the reputation of 'Cottonopolis' as Manchester and its environs were known. A newspaper cutting of 1894 reported, with an impressive display of local pride and with a cavalier disregard for ancient chronology, that 'The mummy which recently arrived in Liverpool from the land of the Pyramids was consigned to a gentleman residing in the Cotton City. The Ship Canal Passenger Steamship Company's boat 'Fairy Queen', in one of her trips from the Prince's Landing Stage to Manchester conveyed the case containing the mummy and the unique cargo excited considerable curiosity among the passengers. For years to come the mummy will perhaps be pointed out as having been present when one of the Ancient Wonders of the World, the Pyramids, were erected, and also as having been taken along one of the greatest engineering triumphs of the nineteenth century – the Ship Canal.'[21]

---

[20] Notebook in Amelia Edwards' hand c1890
[21] Manchester Examiner, 1894

2. Excavators and benefactors

The late nineteenth century saw a great leap forward in the practice of excavation. At this time, William Flinders Petrie was pursuing a scientific approach to digging and recording. His achievements in this field led him to being known as 'the Father of Egyptology'.

Petrie was responsible for the development of many major museum collections in Britain and elsewhere. The Greater Manchester area became a major beneficiary of the material found as a result of his excavations.

The study of Egyptology and the display of properly recorded Egyptian artefacts could not have developed without the energy, enthusiasm, intellectual interest and, most importantly, the money, of a number of outstanding individuals. Amelia Edwards, a professional novelist living in the Bristol area, was a driving force in the study of Egyptology at the end of the nineteenth century. Her visit to Egypt in the winter of 1873-74, during which she had struck up a friendship with Marianne Brocklehurst, inspired a lifelong passion for the subject. Although she never went back to the country, she became a tireless campaigner on behalf of its heritage. Her observations had convinced her that the wholesale destruction of Egyptian antiquities could only be avoided by proper scientific study and disciplined excavation. As a result she became a moving spirit in the foundation of the Egypt Exploration Fund in 1882. This organisation was to help in the funding of many major projects, including the extensive excavations of WMF Petrie. Its successor, the Egypt Exploration Society continues similar work today. Her famous book 'A Thousand Miles up the Nile', which recorded her experiences, was an inspiration to many potential benefactors, including Jesse Haworth, who was to play the main role in the building up of the Egyptian Collection in the Manchester Museum.

Amelia's visit to Egypt was part of a wider programme of travel and seems to have come about by chance. Her first comments on Egypt underline the importance of the role played by change in major historical events. She says, 'in simple truth we had drifted hither by accident, with no excuse of health or business or any serious object whatever; and had just taken refuge in Egypt as one might turn aside into the Burlington Arcade – to get out of the rain'.[1] After this insignificant start, she soon realised the exciting potential of all that Egypt had to offer as well as the problems related to its heritage. Left unchecked, the depredations of the local people who exploited a growing demand from visitors for antiquities, coupled with the sometimes less than scrupulous activities of European collectors, would destroy the major part of it within decades. Amelia Edwards' work through the Egypt Exploration Fund, supported strongly by R.S. Poole, who was in charge of coins and medals at the British Museum, would help to regularise the flow of exported materials. Its work was both protective and exploratory and the Fund recruited reputable archaeologists to carry out work on selected projects all over Egypt.

The Fund developed a policy of co-operation with the Egyptian Government, who would thereby have first claim on any material excavated. Poole's colleague at the British Museum, Samuel Birch, who had responsibility for Oriental Antiquities, was not convinced that this was the right way forward and did not give his wholehearted support. This was to have an important result in the field of Egyptology in England, since Amelia became determined that the Chair which she eventually endowed at University College London, with Petrie in mind, was never to be given to an employee of the British Museum. Petrie's own uneasy relationship with the Museum may have encouraged him to work with other benefactors whose donations laid the foundation for the Petrie Museum in London and the Manchester Collection, as well as those at Bolton and Rochdale. His feud with Wallis

Fig. 9 W.M..F. Petrie in 1889

---

[1] Edwards, A.B,1877

Budge, who had complained that the British Museum had been given inferior artefacts, continued throughout Petrie's life. In 1886, Petrie, who was not always an easy colleague himself, became exasperated by the way in which Poole worked at the EEF. He therefore resigned, attempting to involve Amelia Edwards on his side against Poole. Margaret Drower, Petrie's biographer, details the deterioration in his relations with Poole and his subsequent resignation. Petrie left London before the announcement of his departure from the Fund, leaving Amelia to break the news. She would not allow herself to side wholly with Petrie, since she did not wish to jeopardise her personal friendship with the Pooles. 'I cannot bring myself to the heroic sacrifice of the friendship of a family….with whom I enjoy such close and delightful intercourse when I am in London.'[2] Having said this, she did not allow the problem to affect her relationship with Petrie, her last letter to him as secretary of the EEF ends with the words, 'Goodbye, good luck and God bless you. Ever your faithful friend, A.B. Edwards'[3] She proved her faith in him by immediately setting about raising funds on his behalf, so that he could work independently.

In January 1880, having carefully read Amelia Edwards; 'A Thousand Miles up the Nile', Jesse Haworth, a cotton yarn agent from Manchester, and his wife Marianne, took their own expedition to Egypt. Haworth himself said of Miss Edwards' trip that, 'apart from the pleasure of the journey, it was an educational tour and became to them an inspiration and an abiding interest.'[4] Sometime after this, he seems to have begun a correspondence with the author which was to have great importance for Manchester. Letters from Miss Edwards to Petrie reveal a great deal about her character and methods.

On January 19th 1887, Amelia Edwards wrote to Petrie who was keen to pursue his excavations, 'I have a scheme in my head which may come to something - or nothing - but at all counts I will tell you what it is. I have come to know, by correspondence only, a very wealthy and intelligent man (merchant class) who has travelled in Egypt and is enthusiastically fond of Egyptian antiquities. The acquaintance is quite recent - since you left England - but I think from what I have learned of him in this short time that he is a sort of Erasmus Wilson.' Erasmus Wilson whom she mentions here was 'the only companion I had in Egyptological study' until his death in 1884. Clearly she still missed him a great deal. She continues, 'now it has occurred to me that he is just the man who might be glad to undertake the excavation of the labyrinth (she is referring to an area of Hawara mentioned by Herodotus); and if I go on improving the acquaintance, I do not see why I should not succeed in gaining enough influence on him to get him to do it - and to put it in your hands. If he would give £1000 or £2000, leaving you entirely free to spend it as

Fig. 10 Amelia B. Edwards

you might see fit, that would be a task which would suit you exactly - and you it.'[5]

The reference to her target's class says much about her own attitudes, but it was clearly not a problem since his intelligence - not to speak of his wealth - overrode the fact that he represented 'new money' and that he had risen to his present status through the industrial channels of apprenticeship and learning through experience. The letter continues, 'Do not think this is mere moonshine. I am used to working on a scheme of this sort and I do not know if I have often failed - if ever - it is all a question of patience, management and cussedness and I think I have all three requisites. If you like the idea, I will begin tunnelling my mines and laying my gunpowder.' It seems clear from this that anyone who came into her sights stood little chance of resisting her confident and determined campaigns and, indeed on January 24th, only a few days later, she wrote triumphantly that 'the system works! The man is willing to place £300 at your immediate disposal for the purpose of exploring the western valley at Bahr el Molook, or for any object that you and the man think desirable in the way of Egyptian research.' She explains that 'the man' has written to say that he would be glad if Petrie could continue in his accustomed way and offered £500 further. However he

[2] Rees, Joan,1998 p. 37
[3] Amelia Edwards to WFM Petrie, January 19th 1887,
[4] Haworth, Jesse, in JMEOS Journal, 1906 pp. 13-20

[5] Amelia Edwards to WFM Petrie, January 19th 1887

has said quite firmly 'I must ask that my name is not to be mentioned.'[6]

Miss Edwards continues enthusiastically, singing the praises of 'this good and enlightened man'. He has specified that 'you are to employ the money as you may think fit for the cause of science. He does not care for ordinary curiosities, nor for a mummy unless a royal one. He would be delighted if you found an undiscovered Royal Tomb with its contents intact, however he says, 'I have no wish for a mummy unless it might be of historical interest. I have no sympathy whatsoever with the desecration of tombs except for some special and useful purpose.' Perhaps with a novelist's tendency to exaggerate, she continues 'the man is so noble and generous that you will, I hope, feel a pleasure in doing the best you can with the means he places at your disposal for the advancement of historical research.'

In March, Miss Edwards reveals the name of her wonderful benefactor. It is, of course, Jesse Haworth. In the light of her remarks about royal tombs, it seems a shame that Haworth did not live long enough to see the discovery of Tutankhamun, though his wife did. Petrie was at first a little cautious about 'being bound to an individual' but was reassured by Miss Edwards, 'Mr Haworth is a millionaire. He would never send anything to an auction.' In August she assures Petrie that Haworth will offer any reasonable amount so that he can finish the excavation. 'His desire is to serve you and science. He wants nothing for himself. He would, of course, be pleased with any elegant and choice thing in a small way that you might press upon him.'

The working relationship between the men, with the inclusion of a third party, London businessman Martyn Kennard, seems to have prospered and when the Haworths met Amelia Edwards and Petrie in person, a real friendship developed. Petrie visited the Manchester area in the summer of 1887 to see the Jubilee Exhibition and met both Jesse Haworth and Rev. Aquila Dodgson of Ashton under Lyne. He wrote about his visit to Miss Edwards who replied, 'what you tell me is just what I imagined of both families, but it is a great comfort to find that they are all so nice and so simple in their ways. Their letters all round, husbands' and wives' show a charming hospitality and great intelligence.'

Jesse Haworth and Martyn Kennard financed Petrie's wide-ranging excavation projects in Egypt over a number of years. During this time he dug at a number of major sites all over Egypt including the Middle Kingdom workers' town at Kahun and the whole area round the pyramid of Hawara. Naturally these produced a huge variety of artefacts which were then shared out. The system was that the Egyptian authorities, based at Boulaq, later the Cairo museum, kept what they wanted, then authorised the export of the rest. In the case of the Haworth - Kennard excavations, these would be shared out three ways.[7] Writing from his home

at Woodside, Bowdon, on October 10[th]1887, Haworth gave his provisional assent to a method of sharing out the items brought to England by Petrie. 'As three parties are concerned I think there is nothing for it but to make, as you suggest, 'a common stock' of the results of your explorations and see how it works.' Haworth pointed out that he had not much room to form a collection and that he did not want to be thought of as a dealer in antiquities. It seems clear from this comment that at this stage Haworth had no clear plan of what to do with his share and was anxious not to seem to have a commercial interest in what he received. A draft reply to Jesse Haworth in Petrie's hand in the archive of the Petrie Museum in London shows that Petrie was well aware of Haworth's wish to retain a low profile. It was very much in his interest to respect his wishes. He wrote, 'I fully understand and appreciate your wishes about your connection with the subject. I have not mentioned your name to anyone in this affair and shall not do, either now or in connection with the things found. My own aim, as you know is historical results; and if Mr. Kennard as he says is quite willing to join in such research it seems as well that he should co-operate with us. I shall not mention at Boulaq what resources I have, nor where they come from, it is sufficient that a friend of mine wishes to aid in such work.'

Kennard's own view of his participation in the arrangement was that he would have preferred to work with a view to finding objects of interest, but he also found that 'the historical question is also so superlatively interesting I am quite prepared to advance £200 or £250 towards your explorations in that direction, and if your friend is willing I should co-operate with him, you may depend on me for that sum. I quite agree with you, our interests should be identical, and if I and your friend advance equal sums, and it is understood we three divide any objects of interest that may be discovered; there can be no confusion of interest, particularly if the objects are divided into three shares and drawn for by lot.' A few days later, while on a fishing trip, he sent a letter confirming his support saying, 'I am happy to feel I have an opportunity of adding my mite in unearthing the ghosts of ancient history.' This letter goes on to show that Petrie benefited in other ways too, suggesting a link of friendship as well as a business connection. Kennard wrote, 'we have had some rain at last and the river is good order and I am off to try my luck with the salmon. I am glad the fish reached you safely and in good condition.' All credit must be given to the Victorian postal service for its efficiency.

Petrie's intentions were clearly stated. He confirmed the tripartite arrangement and promised to undertake to attend to the removal to London of all small antiquities that might be found; on the understanding that they should be exhibited for one or two months together in England if he should wish to do so. Any large statues and objects found would be treated like the small antiquities; but the cost of their transport would be borne by the recipient

[6] Amelia Edwards to WFM Petrie, January 19th 1887
[7] Jesse Haworth to Petrie, 1888

Miss Edwards was personally involved in some of the decisions regarding the distribution of artefacts. The relationship with Haworth was well under way when in 1888 Petrie wrote to her, 'I have sent Mr. Haworth the Sealed List. His choice is made. He wishes one to act as his agent in the distribution as I offered to do.' It is clear that his wife, Hilda, was also involved in the apportioning. At her prompting he asked whether Miss Edwards might be satisfied with only a portrait for her University Collection or whether there might be something else she might wish for. A few days later, Petrie wrote to tell her that both Mr Haworth and Mr Dodgson had been through the finds. 'Manchester will have a very fine portrait of a mummy, the mummy in wooden coffin but I could not get Mr. H. to decide on the portraits till Mrs Haworth and you should see them and state both your wishes. So far five of Mr. Kennard's and one of Mr. H's are promised to the National Gallery. I hope a couple more will go from Mr. Haworth, three fine mummy portraits are going to BM from Mr. Kennard.' This letter refers to the fine portrait mummies found by Petrie at Hawara. Kennard had actually watched the excavation of some of these in person, but Haworth always remained at a distance. In August 1888 Amelia wrote to Petrie, 'I should think both Mr Haworth and Mr Kennard will gladly give to the National Gallery - though I think Owens College Museum in Manchester should have one portrait specimen, considering it has just started and that all Mr H's money has been made in Manchester, don't you?'

Petrie's troubled relationship with the British Museum surfaced when it came to the allocation of these fine Graeco-Roman portraits from the Fayoum. Instead of giving them to the Egyptian Department, he persuaded the keeper of Classical antiquities, A. S Murray to receive examples of the Hawara portrait mummies into his department instead of giving them to his much disliked colleague, Wallis Budge. In his own words he said that he had 'screwed up Murray to the sticking point' of taking them as 'fresh paintings of Greeks, leaving Budge to whistle for the mummies' A further remark shows how things could have turned out differently, 'I had looked to making the Egyptian Department home for all my type collections and I am cut out of it. There would have been a magnificent series of mummies of all kinds for it from this year's work. But I cannot bring myself to go and make friends with Budge after all he has done. If they only had a gentleman there one could put up with a good deal'.

While this arrangement was producing excellent examples of Egyptian artefacts, Amelia Edwards and her associates were working tirelessly to raise further funding and to encourage public interest. Jesse Haworth had a high opinion of her qualities, 'she was a remarkable woman, possessing not only literary skill, but also great natural ability.' He recognised that she was 'virtually the founder of the Egypt Exploration Fund and, until her death, was its vital force in organising and developing its usefulness.'[8]

She wrote to Haworth in 1887, 'the difficulty in raising funds for each year's work is enormous. To raise them, I sacrifice my life's work and my private earnings.' This comment reflects the views of many of her friends, including her companion in later life, Kate Bradbury who felt that she was wearing herself out by her devotion to the cause. The fact that she kept a personal eye on the way in which Egyptology was reported in the press is illustrated by a letter from her to the Times newspaper in 1888,[9] in which she points out a mistake which has been made in an earlier report. She informs the readers that it was Jesse Haworth of Bowdon, Cheshire, the same who last year 'enriched the British Museum with the famous throne chair of Queen Hatshepsut', and not, as reported, Martyn Kennard, who had presented the National Gallery with one of the finest of the Hawara portraits found by Petrie.

Both Amelia Edwards and the Petries paid regular visits to the Manchester area and became well-acquainted with Mr and Mrs Haworth and their circle of friends. Miss Edwards came to lecture many times as did Petrie. In 1887, under the auspices of the Royal Manchester Institution, Miss Edwards lectured in the Mayor's Parlour at the Town Hall on behalf of the EEF. This lecture appears to reflect one of the great motivating factors which encouraged the development of Egyptology, an interest in the content of the Bible. A letter appeared over a period of several days early in 1888 in three Manchester Newspapers, the 'Manchester Courier', 'The Examiner and Times' and the 'Manchester Guardian' about this lecture. The writers request a chance to bring the content of the lecture to public notice through the columns of these newspapers since the lecture had been oversubscribed so many people may have missed the chance to hear it. After a summary of the work carried out under the auspices of the EEF by such men as Naville in 1883 who believed he had identified Pithom - Succoth in the Delta, one of the famous 'treasure cities of the Bible' built by Hebrews under Ramesses II, mention is made of Petrie's discovery of Taphanes referred to in the Book of Jeremiah. This information is clearly aimed at capturing the interest of those many Victorian citizens whose most earnest wish was to prove the historical authenticity of the Bible amongst whom was Haworth himself. Miss Edwards had mentioned this fact in one of her letters whilst she was in the process of securing his support for Petrie's work.[10]

The underlying motivation for this letter is revealed when the writers conclude with an appeal for subscribers to EEF. There had been no Manchester subscribers prior to Amelia Edwards' visit in the winter of the previous year and the letter writers make an unashamed effort to trigger feelings of civic pride amongst the local wealthy industrialists. 'We feel very strongly that a society which does such work.... deserves the hearty support of the whole British public and when we know that the Museums of Bristol, Liverpool, Edinburgh and other large provincial cities have already received donations of valuable antiquities in return for

---

8 Haworth, Jesse, in JMEOS Journal, 1906

9 Times newspaper, September 1st 1888, Issue 32480
10 Offprint of letter to press1888,

liberal local subscriptions we cannot but hope that our own city, 'liberal, enlightened, art-loving Manchester', will now come to the front and by contributing generously to the funds of this society establish a claim to some share in the treasures of the great temple of Bubastis.'

The letter is signed by Marianne Haworth of Woodside, Bowdon, the wife of Jesse Haworth, Amelia Edwards' friend, Kate Bradbury of Riversvale, Ashton-under-Lyne, T.C. Horsfall of Bollin Tower, Alderley Edge and A.S. Wilkins of Owens College to add academic weight.

The inclusion of Mr Horsfall's name is interesting. Thomas Coglan Horsfall was a typical follower of the Manchester liberal tradition whose upholders believed it was the duty of the middle classes to guide and ennoble the lives of the ordinary people. In pursuit of this aim he was the founder and owner of the Manchester Art Museum which opened in Ancoats in 1877. He had the active encouragement not only of a number of notable figures in the world of art, including John Ruskin, William Morris and G.F. Watts, but also of Flinders Petrie who advised him on how the collection should be displayed. He was concerned that non-experts should be able to get the maximum benefit from visiting the collection and advised Horsfall to make sure that there were plenty of descriptive labels. He appears to have taken heed of this advice.[11] The museum was not a centre of Egyptology as the University Museum was, but it did possess for a short time at least one mummy, that of Artemidorus. The mummy originally came into Jesse Haworth's own collection in 1887-8 and it was acquired by the Manchester Museum from the committee of Horsfall's Ancoats Art Museum, Manchester in 1888. Horsfall, Haworth and Dodgson were certainly friends with a shared enthusiasm. In 1888 Petrie wrote to Amelia Edwards describing a visit to Manchester. On this visit he met the Armitage brothers (Jesse Haworth's brothers-in-law) and the Horsfalls. 'We all went into Manchester on Saturday morning. Mr Horsfall went over to Ancoats with me and Mrs Haworth. Then we went to Owens and saw the gilt girl with onyxes which Mr H. has given them, besides the fine portrait mummy and the small woman with gilt head'. The visit to Ancoats was presumably to visit Horsfall's Art Museum there. In the afternoon he went over to Ashton-under-Lyne to go over some Egyptian embroideries with Kate Bradbury.

Amelia Edwards herself felt that lecturing was of great importance. After a tour which included lectures in Manchester and Liverpool she wrote to Petrie, 'I do really think it is increasing the interest of the non-scientific public in Egypt'. Petrie himself lectured in Manchester at least once a year but he was always determined to retain his independence from any organisation. A problem arose on one of his visits in the late summer of 1891 when this came into conflict with more formal organisations. He wrote to Amelia Edwards that he 'had a full audience (about 250) who seemed to take every point with the utmost attention.

Boyd Dawkins (of the University) and Haworth palavered on it after.' However, all was not well as he continues, 'was much annoyed at the two speakers both claiming attention for the Fund and proud of my work! They avoided saying that I was working for the fund but used me as a stalking horse to push the fund. This is discreditable, but I had no time to contradict on the spot as I had to run for the train. Have written to the Manchester Guardian to contradict it.'[12]

This correspondence which continued over several days reveals the difficult side of Petrie's nature and even when Amelia Edwards apparently tried to sort out the problem, pointing out in a letter of October 18th 1891 that the whole problem seemed to have arisen because of 'the inadequacy of the reporting'[13] in the Manchester Guardian, he still appeared aggrieved. A further letter to Amelia Edwards showed his feelings, 'this Manchester incident is most unpleasant. I am extremely sorry that it should have entailed long letters to you and equally sorry for myself. After what you said, of course I accepted it as a sheer mistake. But Professor Wilkens' own letter puts a worse face on it. He disclaims any error on his part. One cannot contradict a man's own version as to what he has said he did not say or what he prints. He never alluded to my earlier work but what he did say very emphatically was 'you cannot show your interest in what has been told you today better than by subscribing to the Egypt Exploration Fund'. There was a general laugh at such obvious touting. He avoided actually saying that my work was the Fund's, but he wholly ignored Mr. Haworth and led everyone to suppose that all that was done for the fund'. According to Petrie none of the labels in the Museum or in the College Courtyard refer to 'the Fund'. This appears to have accorded him some satisfaction.

As a result of Haworth's generosity, the Manchester Museum Collection became one of the best in the country containing, as it did, amongst much else, an extensive collection of material from Kahun, a unique domestic site excavated by Petrie sponsored by the tripartite consortium and a few years later, the complete tomb assemblage of the Two Brothers from Rifeh, also one of Petrie's major excavations. This Middle Kingdom tomb contained some remarkable artefacts including model boats. It also contained a chest of canopic jars, the contents of which would later be the subject of scientific study. The fine coffins of the two brothers were contained in a wooden chest.

Kennard's share or that part of it which had not yet been allocated, as some of it was, to the Ashmolean Museum, was, according to Petrie, sold off after his death in 1911. A copy of Petrie's autobiography in the John Rylands Library has been annotated by an unknown hand, possibly that of Mary Shaw, a later curator. A footnote here reads 'much of the share of Mr Kennard during one year's work at Kahun came to Manchester.'

---

[11] Kidd, Alan J. & Roberts K. W. Eds. 1985

[12] Petrie to AB Edwards
[13] A B Edwards to WF M Petrie

Fig. 11 Upper part of the Two Brothers' coffins

During the course of his excavations of a variety of important sites Petrie associated with a number of major personalities in the Egyptological world, several of whom had connections with the Manchester area. One such was Frank Llewellyn Griffith. He had written to Petrie in 1884 asking if there was any chance of working with him in Egypt. This young man, who had no financial means of his own, had been studying the ancient Egyptian language and was already quite proficient in the subject. Petrie was impressed by him and a scholarship was arranged by Amelia Edwards so that he could accompany Petrie on his next expedition.[14] Griffith was later to become closely connected not only with the University of Manchester but also with the Egyptophile cotton magnates of the area. In 1896 he married Kate Bradbury the daughter of Charles Timothy Bradbury of Ashton-under-Lyne and friend of Amelia Edwards. This alliance was to have important consequences for scholarship in Egyptology.

Interest in Egyptology in Manchester was also fostered by the Manchester Egyptian and Oriental Society. This was founded in 1912 by the amalgamation of two earlier groups, the Manchester Egyptian society formed in 1906 and the Manchester Oriental society formed in 1910. Its declared objectives were to discuss questions of interest with regard to the languages, literatures and archaeology of Egypt and the Orient, to help the work of excavating societies in any way possible and to issue, if possible, a journal. These journals provide a clear insight into the membership of the society and the scope of its interests. The original Vice-Presidents included, alongside two bishops, those

of Lincoln and the Roman Catholic Bishop of Salford some significant names in Egyptological scholarship. Two notable names are those of Grafton Elliot Smith, the anatomist whose large collection of Nubian skulls is still providing an important source of information for modern researchers, and A. H. Gardiner the Hieroglyphics expert. The society's foundation coincided with the opening of the new museum extension built to house the Egyptian Collection funded by, and named after, Jesse Haworth, as might be expected, his name appears in the list of Vice-Presidents. Amongst the membership, along with the wives of Haworth and Elliot Smith, other notable names appear. John Barlow and Annie Barlow, benefactors to the Egyptian collection in Bolton and Mrs Robinow, whose husband's collection helped to supplement that in the Manchester Museum, were also members. Professor Canney and Winifred Crompton became the society's secretaries.[15]

The Journal of the Society reported each lecture presented in detail. The first, as befitted the importance of Manchester, was delivered by Petrie in person and was a thorough survey of Egyptian amulets. Elliot Smith delivered the second lecture in which he reported the latest excavations by Quibell. The third lecture of 1912 was on the subject of links between Crete and Egypt, still a subject of interest today. The fourth was perhaps the most interesting of all, a summary of the Progress of Egyptology in Manchester delivered by Haworth himself. The account of this meeting includes a vote of thanks to Mr Jesse Haworth and

---

[14] Drower, Margaret, 1995 p. 85

[15] Journal of Manchester Egyptian and Oriental Society Report 1911-1912

Professor Elliot Smith who had given a lecture on Reisner's excavations at Giza. Professor Boyd Dawkins laid special stress on the advisability of following up a suggestion made by Mr Jesse Haworth that popular lectures should be given in the museum at suitable hours. In 1913 the Society passed a resolution to hold a regular series of lectures in the Museum thus setting a tradition of providing education and fostering enthusiasm amongst ordinary people which has continued to this day. Over the next few years, the Society continued to present lectures on Egyptology but, in line with the interests of many members, there were also those which covered Biblical matters and other aspects of Middle Eastern archaeology.

The annual Journals contained news of members, often in the form of obituaries. The death of Haworth in 1920 was naturally marked by a detailed account of his life and his contribution to Egyptology in Manchester. Sometimes, less prominent figures' roles were acknowledged. Dr Ronald Burrows who died in 1921 had been Professor of Greek at Manchester University some years before. His contribution was acknowledged by the Society. He had settled in Manchester when the Egyptian collection was housed in an ill-lit attic. He worked on the artefacts and was a prime mover in trying to hasten the building of the new extension to house the Egyptian collection as a member of the organising committee. He also urged the appointment of a lecturer in Egyptology, a post which had lapsed some time before.[16] Interestingly there is some evidence that Petrie would have liked to set up some more academic scheme in the north of England, probably in Manchester.[17] There is also no doubt that Jesse Haworth believed that there should be a Chair of Egyptology in Manchester, an ambition which remained unfulfilled in his time. The Chair, which now exists, held by Rosalie David, was not established until 2002.

---

[16] JMEOS IX 1923 pp. 5-6
[17] Drower, Margaret, 2006

3. 'A Good and Enlightened Man'

Jesse Haworth, the man who was to become the most important benefactor to the City of Manchester in the field of Egyptology, through his generosity towards Owens College and later, the Manchester Museum, was born in Bolton in 1835. As a young boy he was apprenticed to the firm of James Dilworth & Son, following his elder brother Abraham, who had been indentured at the age of fourteen and whose indenture shows him promising to obey his employers and not cause any hurt or damage to their interests or embezzle their monies, securities, goods or chattels. His father had to promise to feed and clothe him for the whole seven years of his apprenticeship. In return, he was to be paid four shillings per week, rising each year by two shillings, until the seventh year when he would earn sixteen shillings per week. Although Jesse's indenture has not survived, it seems unlikely that its terms would have differed very much from that of his brother.

The firm was a rising star at this time, almost doubling its profits from £1,264 in 1842, to £2,392 in 1850. Its business was as a commission agent selling yarns. The work required an expert knowledge both of cotton staples and of spun yarns as well as a considerable grasp of manufacturing processes and markets. The business was so prosperous in 1854 when James Dilworth died that his son John, the new head of the firm took on Abraham Haworth as his partner. Within only a few years, John Dilworth himself was dead, leaving Abraham in charge. Abraham took his brother Jesse into partnership and the firm continued to prosper.[1] The firm retained its original name, but was largely controlled by the Haworth family well into the twentieth century. It was typical of many cotton magnates that they had risen through the firm from humble beginnings.

By the 1870s the brothers were comfortably settled in Bowdon, a growing suburb which was becoming fashionable. As active promoters of the cotton business they were, of course, members of the Manchester Royal Exchange and well known in the city. The elder brother, Abraham, had a higher public profile, but their interests and involvement in a wide range of activities were similar. When Abraham died in 1902, his eminence led the Manchester Guardian to devote a whole leader to him. It is not too far-fetched to apply some of the achievements attributed to him to his younger brother who had similar views and interests. The newspaper highlighted the upbringing of the Haworth boys in the Mancunian Liberal tradition, asserting that their 'political convictions were formed in the school of Cobden and Bright'.[2] The prosperity of the Haworth

family grew despite the vicissitudes of the cotton industry at the time of the American Civil War. It is a measure of the liberal views of the Manchester cotton men, of whom the Haworths were typical, that they did not support the cotton producing (and slave owning) southern states.

The religious background of the Haworth family had important consequences for them. Jesse's father was a member of the Hope Congregational Church in Salford, where John Dilworth, and possibly his father, was a member. This could well have been the reason why the young Haworths were readily taken into apprenticeship at James Dilworth & Son. It is also possible that the link with this church made a connection with the Armitage family. Sir Elkanah Armitage, a notable local figure lived at Hope Hall in Pendleton, near to the Hope church. He was a cotton spinner and a JP and was a generous subscriber to chapel building and to Mansfield College in Oxford, set up for nonconformist students. Abraham Haworth was also to become a subscriber. A great niece of Sir Elkanah, Marianne Armitage, was to marry Jesse Haworth and her brother, the Rev. Elkanah Armitage, besides being a Congregational minister and scholar, became an Egyptophile.

The closeness of nonconformist society in the late nineteenth century was partly the result of the disabilities under which dissenters had laboured for centuries. They had been refused burial in consecrated ground, forced to pay church rates and refused entry to the universities. Interestingly, the University of Manchester was never an exclusive establishment and allowed dissenters free access. This may have encouraged local benefactors in their giving. Although these restrictions were gradually being lifted, their effect was still felt in the dissenting community and this led to a strong bond being forged between its members. Intriguingly the Anglican St. Margaret's Church on Dunham Road was built with the intention of serving the rich residents of Bowdon. Instead, the Bowdon Downs Congregational Church attracted the support of men like Abraham and Jesse Haworth who lived in the Green Walk at Hilston House and Woodside respectively.

The evidence for Jesse Haworth's religious interests is clear. He and his wife Marianne were keen supporters of their Chapel and may even have met there. Marianne's grandfather, Ziba Armitage, her father William and her brothers, Elkanah and William were all involved in church meetings from 1860 onwards. They lived in Altrincham at Townfield House and derived their wealth from cotton. In 1869, Abraham Haworth, his wife, and his brother, Jesse all transferred their church membership from

---
[1] Dilworth's, James Dilworth and son (no date) p. 6
[2] Manchester Guardian, 1902

Fig. 12 Hilston House, home of Abraham Haworth

Fig.13 Bowdon Downs Congregational Church:

Eccles Congregational Chapel to Bowdon Downs.[3] Jesse was soon actively involved, acting as a delegate to the Congregational Union of England and Wales in 1874. In 1876 he was elected Deacon. Incidentally, Max Robinow, who also collected Egyptian antiquities, which were presented to Manchester Museum after his death, was a neighbour on Green Walk.

Haworth's interest in Egyptology was certainly partly inspired by and interest in proving the truth of the Bible. In his own house, as his great-niece Barbara remembers, there were Biblical paintings in prominent positions, including one of Daniel in the Lions' Den over the fireplace in the drawing room, which can now be seen in Manchester City Art Gallery. The same great niece recalls her sense of pride when, on a school visit to the Museum in the 1930s, she realised that the building housing the Egyptian Collection bore her surname.[4] The religious interest is further shown by the entry for Woodside in the 1891 census. Jesse and his wife had no children, but his nephews and nieces lived just across the road. At the time of the census Jesse was entertaining the Revered David Simmons M.A. who is recorded as a Professor of Theology.

When Jesse died, legacies were specified for both the minister of Bowdon Congregational Church and the former minister, now retired. He also left bequests for the Congregational Union and other good causes. A comment made a generation later about his great-nephew, Sir Geoffrey Haworth, on the occasion of his receiving an honorary degree in 1956 reflects the historic contribution of the Haworth family, 'the Haworths are clearly a menace to the economic well-being of our society: they are willing to work for nothing in a good cause. They seem determined to illustrate the ancient maxim that it is better to wear out than to rust out.'[5]

Apart from his support of the Bowdon Downs Church, Haworth took an interest in contemporary debates and is recorded, in a Times newspaper article of April 1890, as chairing a meeting of the district Liberation Society which was debating the question of disestablishment of the Church of England, partly on the grounds that it could not fulfil its duty to the poor, because of its size. The Liberal Party is said to be about to address this problem, once Home Rule had been dealt with.[6] History shows that this was never to be achieved.

Although Jesse Haworth had wide-ranging interests, he was most notable for his contribution to Egyptology. A visit to the University Museum in Manchester soon proves this, as one enters the Jesse Haworth Building, which houses one of the best collections of Egyptological material in Britain. Not only was the building and its later extension funded through the generosity of Haworth, but much of the collection of Egyptian artefacts was assembled as a result

of his benefactions. His original introduction to Petrie, which came about through Amelia Edwards, resulted partly from his interest in religion. Miss Edwards wrote to Petrie, 'He is a religious man, and if you could throw any light on the Bible as at Taphanes, he would be gratified.' Petrie visited Manchester in 1887 and met the Haworths for the first time, staying with them for two nights before moving on to the Dodgsons in Ashton-under-Lyne, who were old friends.[7]

Haworth's financial support for Petrie during the ten digging seasons which lasted until 1896 was highly significant since it was perhaps, one of the most productive periods in Petrie's long career. Winifred Crompton, writing in the Journal of the Manchester Egyptian Association, after Jesse Haworth's death, pointed out that this was the period when the Graeco-Roman portrait mummies were found, the pyramids of Amenemhat III and Senusert II were identified, the towns of Gurob and Kahun, full of articles of the XIIth and XVIIIth Dynasties were uncovered and the early history of hieroglyphs elucidated. Furthermore, the excavations at Tell el Amarna 'brought a flood of light on that fascinating personality King Akhenaten, the heretic'. Finds at Koptos and important pre-dynastic discoveries at Naqada added further to knowledge. Finally, Theban excavations led to the discovery of the Stela of Merenptah; the only Egyptian artefact ever found which contains a reference to Israel. This last must have been of great delight to Haworth, given his interest in Biblical matters.

The alliance between Haworth, Kennard and Petrie ceased in 1896, but Haworth's interest did not end there. Throughout the rest of his life, until his death in 1920, he continued to be a generous donor to the Egyptian Research account, Petrie's excavation fund, and to educational institutions such as Owens College, the University of Manchester. The Manchester Museum benefited throughout this time from a constant flow of material, which included the contents of the tomb from Rifeh, which arrived in 1907. He was also patron and president of the Manchester Egyptian Society and, with his wife, was a founder member. Petrie and his wife Hilda visited Manchester frequently; they were present at the opening of the Jesse Haworth Building and subsequently made annual trips to see their various Egyptological friends. These friends now included Winifred Crompton, who played a major role in the Manchester Museum and who was secretary of the Manchester Egyptian Society. Hilda Petrie seems to have enjoyed these visits to Manchester, which included lecturing as well as socialising and to which she referred as 'our usual *fantasia* in Manchester'.[8] The opening of the new building was recorded in the Times on October 31st 1912, which reported that after the ceremony, 'Professor Flinders Petrie delivered an address emphasising the importance of the study of Egyptology, with which, he said, the history of man was so closely bound up.'[9]

[3] Bowdon Downs Church book.
[4] Martin, Barbara, Interview 2008
[5] Haworth family 1956 ms
[6] The Times 31st October 1912

[7] Drower 1995 p. 127
[8] Drower 1995 pp. 323-324
[9] The Times 31st October 1912

In the Manchester Oriental and Egyptian Society's first Annual Report, Haworth's paper on 'The progress of Egyptology in Manchester', is described in full. He had, on the table in front of him, a number of artefacts from Petrie's excavations at Hawara in 1887, which included a number of fine textiles. Underlining the connection between Egyptology and the cotton industry, he was keen to point out that 'some of them resemble cloths which are now produced weekly in their thousands in Lancashire'. He traced the history of Egyptology in Manchester to the Jubilee Exhibition and the artefacts placed, by his generosity, beneath the central dome of the Pavilion. He went on to describe the museum collection and expressed a hope that now that the new building had been opened, 'lectures to school-children and others would be arranged more frequently.' He noted that there was a dearth of papyri in the Museum, but pointed out that the purchase of the Earl of Crawford's valuable collection by Mrs. Rylands in 1901 had made Manchester 'immeasurably rich in this area'. The adoption of the John Rylands Library by the Manchester University brought these collections under its aegis.[10]

Despite some reluctance to name individuals, he felt that some must be singled out. He piled lavish praise on Amelia Edwards whose book had so inspired him and then went on to speak warmly of her friend and travelling companion, Kate Bradbury Griffith of Ashton-under-Lyne, sadly now dead. He made the link between her work and the textile samples on display. 'Although it was more than ten years since the pulse ceased to beat in the hands which so carefully cleansed and mounted the embroideries displayed on the table, it was not without a pang that the lecturer and his wife gave them up quite recently, but they felt it better they should be in the new museum.'

Living individuals, which Haworth singled out, included, of course, Petrie himself, on whom he heaped praise for his scientific work. Haworth's talk went on to give credit to some of Petrie's students, the work of men like Quibell, Weigell, Garstang and Newberry are all well-known in the history of Egyptology and several others whom he mentioned had strong local connections. One of these was Dr. F. Llewellyn Griffith, who became the foremost expert in Demotic Egyptian of his day and who married Kate Bradbury, whom he met while he was Reader in Egyptology at the University of Manchester. Another notable individual was Norman De Garis Davies of Ashton, who was sent to Egypt under Miss Bradbury's influence. Haworth pointed out that the fine paintings on the staircase were by Norman's wife, Nina. In particular Haworth stressed that 'the value of Petrie's work had not been in digging up specimens, but in scientific and historical results, which he had tabulated and published fully and carefully.' In the University there were over forty volumes, which had reference to Petrie's archaeological researches. He modestly omitted to mention that some of these owed their presence there to Haworth himself;

Fig. 14 Dr Jesse Haworth in his doctoral robes

even today it is possible to find books on the shelves with bookplates indicating that they were donated by Haworth, and in at least one, there is a dedication to Haworth in Petrie's own hand. In several others, including 'The Hyksos and the Israelite Cities' by Petrie and others and 'The Ramesseum', by J.E. Quibell published by Bernard Quantich in 1898, bookplates announce that it was donated by Jesse Haworth Esq. On page two of the latter, a note acknowledges that 'a considerable part of the Ramesseum was excavated by Dr. Petrie using funds provided by Mr. Jesse Haworth and Mr. Martyn Kennard'.

In 1913, Jesse Haworth was awarded the degree of Doctor of Laws, in recognition of his largesse to the University, but his generosity was to continue for the rest of his life. In 1919, an appeal for funds by the University did not pass Haworth by. His name, with a subscription of £10,000, to be used for museum purposes, heads the list. Although he was unable to attend meetings of the Manchester Egyptian and Oriental Society as his health declined, he did not neglect to support any appeal for funds. His generosity did not cease with his death in 1920 either, since he left important bequests in his will. All his Egyptian antiquities were left to the Museum and a sum of £30,000 was allocated for the building of a further extension, this was opened in 1929 in the presence of his widow Marianne.[11]

Winifred Crompton's tribute after Haworth's death makes some important points about Haworth's approach. She called him 'the pioneer of scientific donors to archaeology just as Petrie has been described as the pioneer of scientific excavators.' At a time when many wealthy men who had collected antiquities, had been responsible for encouraging 'ignorant or unscrupulous persons to destroy priceless

---

[10] Haworth in JMEOS 1912-1913 pp. 13-18

[11] Haworth, J Will.1920

historical evidence in ransacking of sites for saleable articles', Haworth realised that it would be better to back trained archaeologists in their work rather than buying from less than scrupulous dealers.   His approach was always that of an honourable man to whom Manchester owes a great debt of gratitude.[12]

---

[12] Crompton, W. in JMEOS 1921 p. 49

4. Scientific society to public access

Throughout most of the nineteenth century, and well into the twentieth there was a fashion for making and displaying collections of 'curiosities'. These might consist of ethnographic items brought home by explorers, stuffed birds, fossils, geological specimens and sometimes even more bizarre items. Specialised collections tended to consist either of natural history specimens or classical items such as coins. Societies dedicated to amassing such items were often founded as Natural History Societies. The Manchester Natural History Society was formed in 1821 and its original collection only contained specimens of geology and natural history. One of the more curious items was Napoleon I's horse which was in the stores until it was returned to the French Emperor, Napoleon III in 1841. This was typical.

The first Egyptian donation to the Society was the mummy of Asru together with her mummy cases in 1825. After this, one or two other Egyptian items were acquired. In October 1825 it was agreed that an Egyptian alabaster tablet whose provenance is unrecorded, should be encased and in April 1828 a Mr Hardman donated a piece of Pompey's Pillar from Alexandria which had been collected by Samuel Street, Mr Sydney Smith's boatswain. If this was a genuine relic it seems amazing that Pompey's Pillar still stands today.

The Natural History Society, as befitted its status in the city, kept minutes of all its proceedings so that the various changes of premises in the city centre are recorded in detail. Their collection was at various times housed in King Street, Peter Street, eventually ending in the building in the city centre which later became the YMCA as the first real Manchester Museum. The society took its responsibilities seriously. Victorian philanthropists with plenty of money saw it as their duty to provide educational opportunities for the masses. The 1856-1857 minute book illustrates this point clearly. 'No opportunity affords so effectual a means of elevating the tastes and pursuits of the working class and the young people of the district as frequent and intelligent resort to an extensive and, comparatively speaking, well-arranged museum of natural history such as that of the society.'[1] The Manchester District Schoolmasters' Association asked the Museum committee in 1846 for free entrance to schoolchildren and advertisements for the collection were put up in public parks and on railway stations, reflecting the wish to attract a wide range of visitors. In 1863 the third edition of 'Visits to the Museum of Manchester' by Dr Thomas Ashton MD (1st edition, 1856), mentions curiosities including an Egyptian

mummy and Sarcophagus of Asru or Asroni, maid of honour to the 20th Pharaoh, daughter of Phasco or Fakso, scribe of Lower Egypt, mother's name Tannto. It seems unlikely that the author read the hieroglyphs himself so he presumably had access to some kind of explanatory label in the museum, however unlike any modern translation of these names.

The number of visitors recorded in 1853 was eighteen thousand but this total had declined drastically by 1863 after the opening of the free Royal Museum in Peel Park Salford, causing anxiety to the committee. In 1861 the Manchester Natural History Society joined up with the Manchester Geological Society. In 1868 the Manchester Natural History Society was dissolved but the collection was found a new home. By this time the new educational centre, Owens College had been established on Oxford Road. Initially the collection was offered to the City Council but it was not interested. Instead of this it was decided to move it into the new College area in 1873, having established that the collections should be available to the students and accessible free of charge. In 1880 Owens College became the Victoria University of Manchester which was joined by the University College of Liverpool in 1884 and the Yorkshire University of Leeds in 1888. Thomas Ashton, a cotton spinner and R.D. Darbishire were largely responsible for the original museum building in 1873, the first of many important links between cotton money and museum interests. The Whitworth Trustees were also persuaded to give much financial help in the early stages.

William Boyd Dawkins sorted the collections of the two societies which were now housed on Oxford Road. He finished this job in 1884. His system was based on Time and Evolution. At that time the major part of the collection was still centred on natural history and though Boyd Dawkins' system of classification allowed it to be introduced, no study of 'the history and culture of mankind' was formally allowed for until Haworth's generosity in donating a large proportion of the Egyptian material which he had acquired from Petrie, whose work he had funded, made it possible. It was only after his financial intervention and his insistence that the Egyptian artefacts should be properly displayed and allocated space of their own that the Museum premises were expanded. On the eighth of June 1888 the official opening of the new museum took place. Thus the Egyptological interest was instrumental in the development of the Manchester museum. Professor Boyd Dawkins resigned as curator in 1889 after twenty years in post, but he continued to be involved in running the museum. W.E. Hoyle, a man with a medical background, was appointed 'Keeper' in 1889.

---

[1] Fildes, George, unpublished manuscript is the source of much of the information in this chapter

Fig. 15 The 1912 extension

His Annual Reports provide a vivid picture of what was happening. At first, entry was restricted to members of scientific and other societies but in 1890 it was thrown open to the general public, although children under twelve were to be accompanied by an adult.

During this period, the Egyptian collection began to grow. Jesse Haworth, who had been sponsoring Petrie's work in Egypt since 1888, donated and loaned many items from Kahun, Koptos, Tel-el- Amarna and many other sites. He was not the only donor at the time. Mr M. E. Robinow is recorded in 1895 as giving two mummies, specimens of Egyptian cloth from Akhmin, a mummified crocodile, the head of a mummy, a mummy cartonnage and two stelae. In 1898 there was a series of lectures on 'Egypt, with special reference to the Museum's Collection'. In the following years he records that Petrie himself gave a series of lectures. In 1900, 240 people attended a lecture on 'The first Egyptian Dynasty.' In 1903 the audience had increased to 350 to hear Petrie talk on 'the Ten Temples of Abydos.' In 1905 attendance at Petrie's annual lectures rose to a figure of 'more than 500.' The increasing interest in Egyptology locally was no doubt encouraged by the excellent and growing Museum Collection. In 1905, Jesse Haworth converted the loan of his collection into a gift.

This generosity presented somewhat of a problem since the space available for its display was woefully inadequate. Despite the purchase of a large iron case from Dresden and the promise of donations towards the purchase of further display cases only half the Haworth Collection could be accommodated. This problem was resolved by the construction of the Museum extension, which came to be known as the Jesse Haworth Building. This was largely financed by his largesse and was opened in 1912. The opening of the new building was attended by Petrie

and his wife, Hilda who were by now regular visitors to Manchester and close personal friends of the Haworths.

Meanwhile, the work of caring for the collection was continuing. A catalogue of Egyptian material was being compiled by Miss A.S. Griffith. This did not appear in print until 1910 but was the product of painstaking attention to detail.[2] Miss Griffith was the sister of Frank Llewellyn Griffith, who had worked with Petrie for many years, had been appointed to a lectureship at Manchester University in 1898 and had made many important translations of papyri written in hieroglyphs, hieratic, demotic, Old Coptic and Meroitic. His wife, Kate Bradbury Griffith had died young and Miss Griffith looked after her brother from time to time.

The appointment of Miss Winifred Crompton as Assistant Keeper of Egyptology in 1910 was the start of a new phase in the growth of the Manchester Museum. For the next twenty two years she oversaw a wide range of activities which included lectures for the public by noted Egyptologists, activities for school groups and the accession of many new additions to the Egyptian Collection. The Museum went from strength to strength.

[2] Griffiths A.S 1910

23

5. Cotton and congregations

Manchester, 'Cottonopolis', reached the peak of its power and influence at the end of the nineteenth century. The city itself was the main base for the cotton dealers and yarn agents, while the towns around its periphery were the centre for spinning and processing cloth. Several of the mill towns, Bolton, Rochdale and Ashton-under Lyne had strong links with Egypt. One result of this was the growth of enthusiasm for ancient Egypt and the involvement of a number of industrialists as patrons of excavations and generous donors to museum collections locally. The cotton trade itself was in the hands of an influential elite who may well have known each other outside business. The names Barlow, Heape, Bradbury and Haworth are associated both with the textile industry and with the building up of one of the best collections of Egyptian artefacts outside London. These major industrialists were members of the Royal Exchange in Manchester and could be seen in their morning coats and top hats on their way to do business and to collect the latest gossip from each other.[1] At the height of the industry, many of them built themselves palatial dwellings in the outer suburbs.

A typical representative of this class was John Rylands of Longford Hall, whose fortune was employed after his death by his widow, Enriqueta, in the foundation of the great and remarkable library which bears his name.

This couple epitomise the wealthy, religious, liberal and philanthropic tradition for which Victorian Manchester was famed. From his late twenties, John Rylands approached his work from the perspective of Christian Capitalism. His whole approach, as for many of his contemporaries, was governed by his religious beliefs. Like several of the major players in the story of Egyptology in Manchester, he was born into Congregationalism but his interests were not confined to this denomination. In fact he devoted much of his energy outside his enormously successful business to freeing education from denominational constraints and even found time to compile a broadly based collection of hymns. According to the Dictionary of National Biography, 'he remains a striking example of the innovating entrepreneur inspired by a profound belief in the truths of Christianity.'[2] It was said in 1902 that 'he

---

[1] Haslam Mills, William, 2003 p.xii

[2] Oxford Dictionary of National Biography

Fig. 16 John Rylands

Fig. 17 Enriqueta Rylands

Fig.18 Norman and Nina de Garis Davies

took an especial delight in adding to the studies of the poorer Free Church ministers by gifts of books, and there are many today who preserve a profound gratitude to John Rylands for the helping hand which he extended to them.'[3]

His widow was actively involved in funding not only the Zion Chapel in Stretford but also the Salford Central Mission and she left £10,000 to the Lancashire Congregational Union.

John Rylands himself was not directly involved in the development of Egyptology, though his widow acquired a number of important papyri for the new library, opened in 1899, which she endowed in his name. If he was not himself an Egyptology enthusiast, he is almost bound to have known some of the other local businessmen who were; since several of them shared his interest and enthusiasm for free church religious practice.

Jesse Haworth, the generous benefactor of the University Museum was another Congregationalist. Living as he did, in the wealthy suburb of Bowdon, he attended the prestigious Bowdon Downs Church. This was an equal, possibly a rival, of the Albion Church over in Ashton-under-Lyne where there was a strong caucus of Congregationalist businessmen involved in the textile trade who were also Egyptology enthusiasts. One of the reasons for this interest was, of course, the desire to use the developing study of Egyptology to prove the truth of the Bible. This was indeed one of Flinders Petrie's original motivations for excavating in Egypt. As the nineteenth century drew to its close, these people all became not only colleagues and fellow-enthusiasts but also personal friends. The circle was completed by the friendship between the daughter of

one of the Ashton magnates, Charles Timothy Bradbury, and Amelia Edwards herself. Kate Bradbury and Amelia Edwards travelled together and exchanged prolific correspondence not only with each other but with a wide range of other interested parties.

The influence of religious activity at this period is apparent in the building of new churches, especially of the Congregational persuasion, using money made in the textile industry. Many successful businessmen were happy to use their wealth in the endowment of places of worship. In 1868 Sir Elkanah Armitage, one of these Congregational worthies gave a fund-raising lunch and raised the huge sum of £17,350 and a committee was set up to organise the building of churches.[4] His extended family which included Rev. Elkanah and his sister, Marianne Haworth, were great enthusiasts who became friendly with many other like-minded people, which included the Ashton group of Egyptophiles who were involved in 'a fearful outbreak of Egyptology'. This was centred on the Albion Congregational Church, which is still an important landmark in the town. An outstanding example of Congregational influence at this period, Albion is a fine Gothic church which, apart from having no central altar, closely resembles a mediaeval parish church. It was erected just across the road from the Anglican parish church, it seems as a rival to it. Lord Stamford who owned most of Ashton refused to allow any non-conformist place of worship on his property, so when this particular parcel of land became available from a private source, the congregation seized the opportunity to buy it and build. This is an interesting illustration of the gulf between old money, and new industrial money, which was to be of such advantage to the local development of Egyptology.

---

[3] The John Rylands Library, Manchester. July 1902

[4] Robinson, W. Gordon,1955

Fig.19 Part of Aquila Dodgson's collection now in Leeds

Albion became the centre of culture in the town, having a popular Literary Society and holding frequent lectures, some of them by members who had travelled in Egypt and the Levant.[5]

As one of the prime motivations for an interest in Egyptology was linked to the Bible, it is not surprising to find that some of those involved were ministers of religion. Norman de Garis Davis who with his wife, Nina, became leader in the field of recording Egyptian paintings and inscriptions, was for a short time in the 1890s a Congregational minister in Ashton-under-Lyne and therefore part of the remarkable circle. He was certainly a friend of Kate Bradbury, later Mrs Frank Griffith, who seems to have introduced him to Flinders Petrie. He left Ashton for Egypt in 1896 accompanying Petrie and his new wife Hilda on their 'honeymoon' trip through middle Egypt. Later Davis worked as a copyist with Petrie at Dendera in the season of 1897-1898. He met his wife, Nina, in 1906 and they worked together in Egypt until 1939. Between them they recorded, and therefore preserved for posterity, a huge range of tomb paintings at such important sites as Beni Hasan and Amarna as well as the Theban necropolis.[6]

Another minister who became interested in Egyptology in the early 1880s and who pursued a prolific correspondence with many notable Egyptologists was Aquila Dodgson. Although he was a Yorkshire man, born in Hull and was eventually to die in Leeds, he spent much of his time, until 1891, over in Ashton, after finding that his voice would not stand up to the rigours of preaching. He became involved in the textile business and presumably made his fortune, though a letter of July 11th 1891 from Petrie to

Dodgson mentions the latter's 'great catastrophe'. There is no indication of what this could have been, though a reference to insurance suggests that perhaps it was a fire. Petrie comments, 'it will not be a loss without a gain if you are now able to spend your time on using, instead of the making of money'.[7]

Certainly Dodgson had been a collector for some time before this. In October 1882, he was in correspondence with Samuel Birch at the British Museum, about a papyrus which he had acquired from Elkanah Armitage, then a minister in Oldham, and later a lecturer in Rawdon near Leeds. The latter had bought it 'out of the tray of a lad on the island of Elephantine'. According to Frank Griffith (Kate Bradbury's widower) who did some work on it in 1909, writing in the Proceedings of the Society for Biblical Archaeology, it originally had a clay seal attached but this was lost after having been placed in a little crystal box. One of Mr Dodgson's family appropriated the pretty box for another purpose and the seal was lost.[8] In the original correspondence, Birch informs him that this papyrus is a malediction of a mother on her daughter for embracing Christianity.[9] This would have been of great interest to those involved in the various Biblical history societies which existed at the time and it illustrates the common motivation of these religious men. Another letter to Theo Pinches of the British Museum about a Babylonian tablet reflects Dodgson's interest in the Biblical flood story. Later correspondence with Birch, dating from 1882-1885, shows a regular traffic between them, which included antiquities, and hieroglyphic inscriptions requiring interpretation. Evidence suggests that there was an amazing amount of

[5] Moon, Brenda 2005
[6] Strudwick, Nigel

[7] Dodgson Correspondence
[8] Moon, Brenda, 2000
[9] Dodgson Correspondence

Egyptian material in circulation at this period, as collectors sought expert advice on and interpretation of the items they had acquired. Some of Dodgson's collection is now on display in the Leeds Museum, which acquired it with the help of grants from the Heritage Lottery Fund and the Leeds Philosophical and Literary Society, of which Dodgson had once been Secretary, in 2003.

Aquila Dodgson was one of the scholars who addressed the Albion Literary Society on such topics as 'Three of the Pharaohs'.[10] He knew Petrie, who visited Ashton and Manchester regularly. Petrie, writing to Amelia Edwards in September 1888 describes one such visit. In it he mentions that 'at Riversvale (Bradbury's) I had a good afternoon over the embroideries and settled all I had to see about. I saw Mr. Bradbury last year but had not seen Mrs. B before. The Dodgsons were as pleasant as ever, I like Mrs. D's good sense'.

Dodgson also had a regular correspondence with Amelia Edwards, much of which can be found in the Griffith Institute in Oxford. In 1889 she wrote to him in enthusiastic terms. 'My dear sir, you are an ally worth having, and I never cease to congratulate myself on having made your acquaintance.'[11] This letter shows how Amelia Edwards was prepared to help fellow enthusiasts. She describes the process of how to make a squeeze, the most popular means of recording reliefs at that time. She recommends the use of soft, woolly quality paper. This should be damped, dried on blotting paper, then laid over the inscription and patted into the hollows with a fine brush like a toothbrush. A later letter discusses the squeezes which he has made and sent to her. She also mentions a demotic papyrus which was at Warrington. It 'cannot have been translated because Dr Birch did not read demotic - nor did any Englishmen till quite recently. Our friend and student Mr Griffith began to study it.' This is a reference to Frank Griffith who was to become the leading expert on Egyptian texts. This letter ends with a further warm message of appreciation. 'I am extremely obliged for all your kindness...You are rendering a service to science and I shall gratefully acknowledge your aid when I publish the results.'

Dodgson clearly took an active interest in local Egyptological collections. A letter to Amelia Edwards from his home at Limehurst in Ashton dated 1887 describes his visits to Peel Park in Salford. Mr Peart, the museum's curator, 'kindly opened his case and assisted me most genially for three hours in taking squeezes and copying hieroglyphs.' He goes on to detail the inscriptions on several artefacts such as coffins and ushabti figures in the museum. This letter tells an amusing story of the rescue of a female coffin from the beer cellar of a local pub. According to Dodgson, the publican was a clown at a theatre who was anxious to keep the interest of his audience by any available means. He decided that if he were to get a mummy and bring it out as a ghost on the stage it would have a striking and startling effect in the pantomime. He

bought this mummy for the purpose, never thinking that he would have to clear it with another not quite so ghostly individual - his wife. When she discovered the presence of this other lady in the house, she took leave of her senses and protested loudly, saying she 'could not sleep o'nights for fright while the mummy was in the house.' The clown then began to fear that she would report him to the police for giving house room to the poor innocent cause of the commotion, which he left huddled among the beer barrels in the basement of his house, whilst he went and begged the curator of the Salford Museum to come and fetch it from there. Dodgson comments, 'to what strange uses may we come - the adventures after death are almost as wonderful as those before - in some instances at least.'

It is clear from this correspondence that Miss Edwards became a close friend of the Dodgsons through their shared interests. At the time of the Manchester Jubilee Exhibition she was in great demand. She was invited to lecture at Owens College on the subject of the EEF, asked by Miss Barlow in Bolton to do the same and hoped to fit in a visit to the Haworths and the exhibition besides. She wrote to Dodgson, 'if I can truly promote the interests of the Fund and of Egyptology, I suppose I must try what I can do but I have promised nothing as yet. I imagine my best way will be to do as Mrs Dodgson so kindly suggests - namely pay my first visit to you and see Manchester from Ashton-under-Lyne, then go to Mr Haworth's and see the exhibition from Bowdon...and then to go on to Mr Horsfall in Liverpool last.' On Mrs Dodgson's advice she appears to have had second thoughts, believing that her health would not stand up to such a gruelling schedule.

A few days later she wrote to Dodgson thanking him for a head. It is unidentified but in the letter she appears excited and convinced that it represents 'Hatasoo', (the early version of the name Hatshepsut) 'the greatest woman of antiquity. It is simply priceless, worth more than Mr Haworth paid for the throne.' She is to send Haworth a pair of eyes in ivory so that he can restore the head before the exhibition and she offers him a crowned uraeus, presumably to place on the statue. These letters, though sent to Dodgson, imply that he and Haworth were by this time in close correspondence. It should be remembered that in those days a letter sent by the morning post could reach its destination before tea.

Later, in 1891, Petrie wrote to Dodgson 'I hope you will come to Egypt next winter and stay with me for a time.' This is around the date of Dodgson's catastrophe but it does not appear to have affected his urge to collect. He apparently asked Petrie for a mummy. Petrie replied that he could get him a plain one for £5 or a fancy one for £10. He then pressed Dodgson for an answer to his invitation. On September 15th he shows his high opinion of Mrs Dodgson. 'If Mrs D. comes, you'll have to live in a tent, but I see no difficulty in the way of a practical person like your prudent wife. I should dearly like to see her instructing a small boy in domestic duties of cleanliness etc. - I look forward to it.' A subsequent letter suggests that if the Dodgsons were to

---

[10] Moon, Brenda 2005
[11] Dodgson Correspondence

Fig. 20 Riversvale Hall

venture into Petrie's world, they would have to put up with somewhat Spartan conditions, as Petrie described his food stocks. 'My stores consist of 1lb of fish, tongue or meat or thick vegetable soup, three quarters of a pound of jam, bread in the country, wholemeal biscuits, Van Houten's cocoa, tea, (coffee in the country), tapioca, (rice and lentils in the country).' No doubt Mrs Dodgson would be reassured to find 'soap, carbolic acid and insect powders' were also included. Several later letters give instructions about where to stay in Cairo, what clothes to bring, how to travel and advice on bedding. In the event Aquila certainly joined Petrie but the record does not say whether Mrs D. accompanied him. Further notes from Petrie were sent to Dodgson in Egypt. One offers advice on how to acquire papyri and how to handle them. Another informs him that 'my friend Mr (Greville) Chester may see you. He is coming up in a small boat alone. If he calls, (as I have suggested), you cannot do better than ask his advice as to values of antiquities'. One hopes that Mr Dodgson found his trip a profitable one.

Aquila Dodgson had friends in the wider Egyptological sphere and with other major players in the area. Rev. Elkanah Armitage and his wife Ella Sophia, gave a number of lectures on Egypt to the Albion Church Literary Society and were close to the Bradbury family of Riversvale in Ashton-under-Lyne. With Jesse Haworth and his wife, Elkanah's sister, Marianne, Elkanah and Ella Sophia went to Egypt in 1880, inspired by Amelia Edwards' book, 'A Thousand Miles up the Nile'. The visit was to have important consequences for the study of Egyptology in Manchester.

The Bradbury family who lived at Riversvale Hall was headed by Charles Timothy. This typical example of a cotton magnate of remarkable character is allocated a whole article in 'Grey Pastures', an unusual little book by Haslam Mills, who attended the Albion Church as a boy.[12] The articles all appeared in the Manchester Guardian between 1912 and 1919. Many of those described in it are given pseudonyms. Charles Timothy Bradbury is named 'Mr Darlington'. He seems to have been a somewhat intimidating man whose intellectual interests were wide-ranging. As a businessman in the cotton trade, he would travel to Manchester every Tuesday and Thursday by first-class train 'not without a suspicion of cotton waste upon his sleeve - for it was a proud feature of our aristocracy that it didn't look it'. This shows a man whose exalted position as managing director of J.H. Gartside & Co. which owned Wellington Mills, Bridge Eye Mills in Dukinfield and Buckton Vale Printworks [13] did not prevent him from taking an active interest in what was happening in the Works.

Amongst other interests he was a Justice of the Peace and chairman of his local parish council for four years. He had an active involvement in the development of the Albion Day Schools, a typical educational project of the day. He also, in common with many cotton magnates, was one of the original promoters of the Manchester Ship Canal which provided a great boost to the cotton trade. He went to Parliament on no less than six occasions to give evidence on behalf of the project.[14] Bradbury was a Liberal Unionist and active Congregationalist but also became interested in Egyptology. When he died, his funeral was conducted by his friend and fellow Egyptophile, Rev. Elkanah Armitage. His daughter, Kate, the only one of his children to reach majority, increased interest in Egyptology in Ashton-under-Lyne through her friendship with Amelia Edwards and her subsequent active involvement in the work of

[12] Haslam Mills, William 2000 pp. 72-73
[13] Unwin, Richard 2008 p. 20
[14] Obituary of C. T. Bradbury, Ashton Reporter, April 19th 1907

the EEF, Petrie's discoveries, and the development of the subject in general.

Ashton was not the only town in the environs of Manchester where Egyptology was the focus of enthusiasm. In other cotton towns around, like Bolton and Rochdale, local industrialists became involved in the building up and display of important Egyptian artefacts. Strangely, Ashton did not have its own collection. Bolton people subscribed to the EEF and the Egyptian Research Account and therefore benefitted from much that was discovered during excavations. The successive curators of the new museum there, William and Thomas Midgley had a particular interest in, and expertise relating to textiles, as might be expected in a town which had very strong connections with Egypt through the cotton trade. Local benefactors in Rochdale used the profits from the woollen industry.

6. A 'woman of great brilliancy'

Fig. 21 Kate Bradbury

The history of Egyptology in Greater Manchester is remarkable for the frequent appearance of highly talented women. One of the first of these to take a prominent role in the field was Kate Bradbury, the daughter of C.T. Bradbury of Riversvale Hall in Ashton, the respected cotton manufacturer. In his obituary, the local paper described Kate, who had predeceased him, as 'a woman of great brilliancy' who was 'accounted an authority on Egyptology.'[1] She was a woman of wide interests and strong enthusiasms, who not only formed links with that local group of intellectuals who were dedicated students of ancient Egypt, but also extended her circle of contacts to some of the most important names in late nineteenth century Egyptology. When Stuart Poole of the Egypt Exploration Fund visited Riversvale, he was struck by Kate, whom he found to be something of an enigma. He said 'she interests me, as Homer says, awfully. There is a restlessness of an imprisoned genius about her.'[2]

She became a personal friend and companion of Amelia Edwards and was actively involved with the sorting and processing of material sent to Manchester by Petrie from Egypt. Her correspondence with both of these individuals, and their replies to her, provide a vivid insight into what was going on at the time. There are many references to material being sent by Petrie and what became of it on its arrival, often into the Manchester area, having been shipped via Liverpool. In accordance with the major local preoccupation, there was a great interest in the many textile items which came in from Egypt.

Kate was actively involved in the processing of such artefacts. Some of these must have arrived in a sorry condition and Kate took upon herself the responsibility for cleaning them. Describing one consignment she explained, 'those which for their size did not bear the weight of water which they would take up in dealing with them, those stiff with wax and bitumen, and some beautiful and ragged large pieces of surpassing pictorial interest - very frail, in parts very dirty - together with some scraps of silk - Pullars (the dry-cleaning firm) will do for me in my absence. I dare not leave them undone, they would rot.' Modern conservators might wince at the only choice available - either domestic laundry or the dry-cleaners' shop. She continued 'one boxful of very strong pieces our domestic institution - Mary Anne - will deal with, also in my absence. Of the rest which are amenable to hydropathic treatment, the best are done and the same Mary Anne has been trained to finish the remainder.' Mary Anne the domestic, whose surname in the census record is given as Thomasson, was clearly a treasure who could be trusted with such fragile items. The same letter describes the allocation of small items to various people. Kate has given 'a little shirt, a longer shirt, a cap a small piece of yellow silk and a piece of linen darned with coloured wools to the Museum of Fine Art, Boston.' Greenock and Paisley she says 'have both very good museums,' to which she has allocated a small piece of silk and a shirt and cap, 'very damaged'. She comments that 'Mr Dodgson has had some uncleaned rubbish. Poor Mr. Dodgson!'[3]

Petrie, who could be somewhat irascible, was very sensitive to any attempt to acquire samples without his express permission. In 1890 for example, there was a serious misunderstanding about the motives of a Mr Darbishire (whose name was misspelled by Kate until she realised it should be spelt with an 'i' and not a 'y'), of the Whitworth Institute in Manchester. He requested samples of textiles for 'purely scientific reasons.'[4] Following this request, he appears to have visited Kate Bradbury at Riversvale, her home, and made his choice of samples. Kate wrote to Petrie, 'six weeks ago, Mr Darbyshire wrote

[1] Ashton Reporter 1907 April.
[2] Moon, Brenda 2000.
[3] Bradbury to Petrie 1891
[4] Bradbury to Petrie 1891

to me that, with your authority and that of Jesse Haworth, he was able to make a selection from the last batch of Coptic textiles for the Whitworth Institute.' A note inserted here in Petrie's hand reflects his inclination to fly off the handle. It says 'none were Haworth's and never gave him authority to take anything'[5] Kate continued, 'I asked him to wait until I was at home and then to come over and take that which he was to take.' She then described the selection of items. She enlisted the help of Aquila Dodgson, as well as of Petrie. Kate wrote to Petrie, 'on the 16th December, Mr Dodgson and I, Amy helping us by an occasional visit, looked over the contents of eight cases and Mr Darbishire has, out of them, filled one - which is now in his own possession.' She continues, 'in the cases we found a pair of child's shoes (which Mr Darbishire had for the Institute, subject to ratification), glass amulets 'said to be from Gurob' and some little jars in red-ring glaze, likewise pieces of XIX Dynasty tailoring… Mr. Darbishire knows nothing of textiles he says, but he distinguished himself like the 'Heathen Chinee in the game he did not understand' by taking some very good things. Pieces, of greater archaeological than technological interest, I kept back, for all his longing looks, and I shall send things too good to run the risks of water, to Pullars again.'[6]

Following this letter, Petrie wrote directly to Mr Darbishire, 'some time ago I heard from Miss Bradbury with regard to your selection of samples of textiles for analysis of the colours. As I have had no other communication I imagine that there has been some misunderstanding about this subject. I should say that none of those textiles in the eight cases sent last to Miss Bradbury belong to Mr Haworth but only any that she might have left over of previous lots. Those eight cases were all purchased in Egypt by myself and a friend, his cases being marked F; and I am not at liberty to give away anything of his that is of value.'

Darbishire's response is conciliatory, 'Miss Bradbury has sent to me your note of the 12th of February. I am sorry if any misunderstanding has arisen about your textiles and especially as to the ownership of the eight cases. I understood we were dealing with property of which Mr Haworth at least disposed, and I further understood from him that I might borrow textile specimens for exhibition at our Whitworth Museum here. The enclosed makes things clearer - there is no question of appropriation but only of a loan exhibition. So supposing, I selected under Miss Bradbury's eye some specimens of garments and a good many small pieces of textile or embroidered stuff and some pieces of coloured stuff to take samples off, for analysis. I have been working for some time on the smaller pieces in cleaning and displaying them for exhibition, but everything is in my room and I can, and of course will, return all as you or your friend may desire, except what shall go to Dr Schunk and Dr Wiedermann.'[7] Fortunately the misunderstanding seems to have been ironed out and the Whitworth Art Gallery collection nevertheless

still contains some outstanding textiles from Petrie's excavations.

Sometimes the consignment was in a damaged state upon receipt. One of these put Kate in the position of finding 'myself obliged to work the lot off in the limited time at my disposal seeing that the cakes of salt or Natron had wetted everything and that there was much mildew when I first examined the contents of nine cases.' This is perhaps, not surprising considering the long journey they would have made by sea. Petrie wrote to Miss Edwards about the allocation of the various items, 'of course you will come in for some of the spoils from Riversvale. Miss Bradbury is to make up your Akhmin set as complete as any out of the Fayoum. I have asked her to make up four sets without saying who they are for. The most complete is for herself, the others for Mr Dodgson, Mrs Haworth for one of her brothers and for Oxford. Of course the above division is after (1) the most complete set for Manchester, (2) fine pieces for Mr Haworth and Mr Kennard.'

At this time Amelia Edwards was in a delicate state of health following surgery and had been staying with Kate at Riversvale. Kate confessed to Petrie 'Miss Edwards had had a few small pieces of last season's. She picked them up while I was going over them last October and I had not the heart to suggest that she should lend them till your return. They are mostly bits of bordering and one or two pieces she means to give to the American artist in Rome. None are unique.'

Kate Bradbury had many friends and contacts, some of them based in Oxford. Though she was not, in common with most of her female contemporaries, the recipient of a university education, she was clearly of an intellectual cast of mind. She had correspondents who were involved in academe. One of these seems to have been the beneficiary of one of Petrie's finds. In a letter to Petrie, Kate says, 'Somerville Hall, Oxford, viz the Principal, and my friend Miss Maitland has one of your bought, eighty-eight to eighty-nine shirts which I had given up hoping to mend into anything like integrity.'

It is possible that Kate met Amelia Edwards through her Oxford contacts and they became firm friends. There is much evidence of their spending time at each other's houses. In 1890 the two went on a lecture tour of the United States. Kate wrote a complete account and her descriptive journals are in the Griffith Institute in Oxford. Towards the end of the trip, Amelia Edwards, whose constitution was never robust, had a nasty fall and broke her arm. Having an indomitable spirit, she insisted on delivering all the lectures she had promised, which seems to have weakened her further, and, as her health began to fail, Kate became her constant companion and support. Shortly after their return from America, Amelia underwent surgery for a breast problem. She never really recovered and became even more dependent on Kate's support. Kate wrote to Petrie, 'Yesterday I took my dear Miss Edwards as far as Birmingham on her way to Bristol. And now she is away from me for the first time since I joined her in London

[5] Petrie note on Bradbury to Petrie 1891
[6] Bradbury to Petrie 1891
[7] Darbishire to Petrie 1890

last July. I shall go to her in a week'. Kate's anxiety for her friend is very apparent, 'she is very weak and entirely helpless and the weight of my heart about her wakes me at nights. She has been here a good deal, and lastly for a month, making this the centre of a Northern Lecture Tour, which she has repaid herself for the operating surgeon's fee. Could she have remained here for a long rest, unharassed by domestic worry, the lecture tour would have done her no harm, but mentally good. Travel always pleases her, and to be doing something, be among the living again was happiness.'[8]

A further letter to Petrie provided him with an update on Amelia's progress, 'the doctors all agree that there is not even a threatened return of the mischief which was not fully established before the operation. The case was a peculiar one it seems and its very peculiarities made it more hopeful. But she is much aged and weakened and very helpless, yet I am thankful that her depression is less. That I dreaded, considering her hereditary tendencies and her ways of looking at things.' This shows a sensitivity and insight on Kate's part.

Amelia Edwards caught a chill, which turned into a bout of influenza, while supervising the unloading of a consignment on behalf of the Egypt Exploration Fund. Although she recovered enough to plan a new lecture tour in the north of England, she succumbed to bronchitis and possibly to the after-effects of the earlier operation and died, in April 1892. Kate Bradbury and Petrie sorted out her Egyptian collection, going through the house and distributing her Egyptian artefacts.[9] A letter card postmarked August 1892 to W.M. Flinders Petrie makes the first mention of the man who was to become Kate's husband, Frank Llewellyn Griffith, and says 'I want Mr Griffith to have something of Miss Edwards, (failing you, she wanted him to be her first Professor. It will be curious if he joins you, as you proposed).'[10] Petrie and Kate went to visit Amelia Edwards' grave in Henbury churchyard near Bristol. Looking at the grave, they decided that Amelia's Egyptological interest should be marked. As a result, a large stone *ankh* sign, the Egyptian symbol of life, was placed on the ground within the grave area. The epitaph on the obelisk reads, after her name, 'who by her writings and her labours enriched the thought and interests of her time'.

After Amelia's death, Kate continued to work tirelessly in the cause of Egyptology. She wrote many articles for various publications including the Manchester Guardian, The Manchester Examiner, The Times and The Academy. She also translated the first few chapters of Maspero's work on Egyptology.[11]

She may have met Frank Griffith when they were both members of the EEF Committee where they appear to have worked well together. Griffith was rather a shy man

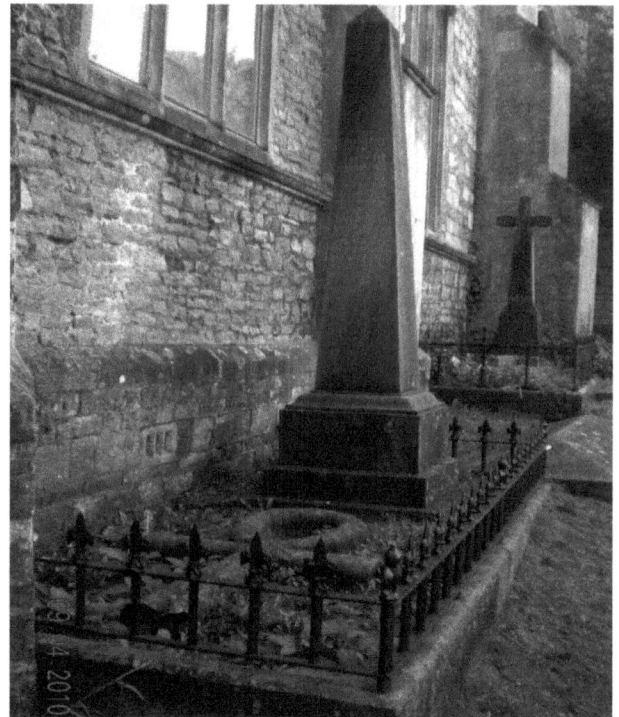

Fig. 22 Amelia Edwards' grave in Henbury churchyard

who asked Petrie's advice before plucking up the courage to propose to her.[12] They married in 1896 and her father settled a large fortune on her. Their happy union was prematurely shortened by Kate's somewhat unexpected death. She had undergone surgery, for what was described as 'an internal malady'. She had apparently begun to recover and the couple took a house in Silverdale, hoping to improve her health but she died a few months later, in March 1902. Two notable mourners at her funeral were Mrs Jesse Haworth and Miss Annie Barlow, of the well-known Bolton textile family, who was an Egyptology enthusiast and benefactress.

Griffith, now a widower, was left living with his father-in-law at Riversvale. In 1909 when he had left Manchester for Oxford he was married again, to Christine Cobban Macdonald who died in 1937.[13] By the terms of his will the inheritance from both of his marriages played an important part in the establishment of the Griffith Institute in Oxford, now an important academic institution specialising in Egyptology. Like Mansfield College, the Oxford Congregational College, the Griffith Institute benefitted extensively from the cotton wealth of Greater Manchester.

[8] Bradbury to Petrie 1892
[9] Bradbury to Petrie 1892
[10] Ashton Reporter 8th March 1902
[11] Drower, Margaret 1995

[12] Unwin, Richard, 2007 p. 36
[13] Griffith Institute

Fig.23 Kate Bradbury Griffith with her husband, Frank Llewellyn Griffith

7. Egyptian cotton and the Lancashire towns

The links between cotton magnates who lived and worked outside the centre meant that interest in Egyptology was not restricted to the City of Manchester itself. Important contributions to the development of Egyptology made by residents of Ashton-under-Lyne have already been explored. The work of local individuals such as the Bradburys and Rev. Dodgson was significant, but there is no major Egyptian collection in the town. In the cotton towns of Bolton and Rochdale however, it was rather different, there, the Egyptian enthusiasts made a physical contribution in the shape of donations to Egyptological causes. In common with other Lancashire cotton towns the predominant industries were those relating to textiles. Before about 1860, most cotton came from America, but the cotton famine at the time of the Civil War led to a major change.

Egypt became the new focus for the trade in the latter part of the nineteenth century and trade developed rapidly, since the long-staple Egyptian cotton produced high quality yarn. The industry in Bolton was dominated by 'the aristocratic spinners of Egyptian cotton.'[1] The connection with Egypt led some of these businessmen to use Egyptian themes in their advertising. Mill Hill Spinning Co. Ltd., produced a four page leaflet to advertise its 'Carded Egyptian Yarns', lavishly adorned with Egyptian motifs and hieroglyphs and which included imaginary scenes of ancient Egyptians sorting cotton, spinning and weaving.

By 1919, virtually all the cotton produced in the Nile Valley was spun in Bolton mills. It was claimed at the time that it was the influence of cotton magnates such as the Heatons and the Crosses that persuaded the government of the day to invest in large-scale irrigation schemes. In a typical outburst of civic pride, the industry claimed that 'Bolton's enterprise has had a civilising influence, inasmuch as it has helped to make deserts fertile, and so find useful employment for people far beyond its own boundaries.' Certainly the town was pre-eminent in the production of very high quality yarns, some of which were so fine that one pound of cotton could be made to produce a thread stretching one hundred miles. In the early 1920s there was an economic downturn in the spinning business but the Egyptian section was relatively stable throughout it. 'The happiness of the Egyptian section is quickly explained. In Egyptian there is no competition worth speaking about'.[2] Even as late as 1955, at least 80% of the cotton used in Bolton came from Egypt and the Sudan.

Naturally, there were strong links between the two places, and many business visits must have been made by local

Fig.24 Egyptian themed advert for a Bolton Mill

people to Egypt, a tradition which stretches back to at least 1843 when Mr Robert Heywood of Bolton recorded his visit to Egypt and helped to stimulate an interest in that country amongst the residents of his home town. Some visitors were not overtly connected with cotton, a diary in the town's archive dates to 1905 and records the visit to Egypt by Assman Granville. His interest seems to have been historical, topographical and Biblical, since he quotes Herodotus and then goes on to relate Alexandria, which he visited, to St. Paul. On his travels he visited underground tombs and passages and pyramids, in which he particularly revelled.[3] It might not be too much of a leap to imagine that he may have been acquainted with Boltonian cotton magnates like the Barlows, who became known for their interest in, and sponsorship of, Egyptian exploration and research. A more recent example of someone who travelled for business reasons is that of Alan Lord, who started work as a machine fitter aged 14 in 1928 and only died a few years ago, aged 90. This was a man who could tell the quality of cotton simply by its feel. His job entailed buying cotton from many sources and dealing in the Exchange, he rose to be a buyer for Barlow & Jones and went to Egypt for the firm, like many another.

In Bolton, Samuel Taylor Chadwick who was a medical doctor from Wigan founded the Chadwick Museum. He had lost his two children in infancy and so he devoted his life, until 1875 when he died, to the care of poor

---

[1] Longworth , James H. 1987 p. 78
[2] Bowker,B, 1928 in Longworth, James H. p. 79

[3] Ms in Bolton Museum and Archive Collection

Fig.25 The Chadwick Museum, Bolton

and deprived children. He also left £5,000 for building a museum, which was eventually built in Queens Park, Bolton and named after him.

This bequest was not without its problems, since the budget of the Library committee, which was in charge of the Museum, proved inadequate to support it. The museum was passed over to the Park and Burial Board Committee.[4] The museum was to acquire a notable collection of Egyptian antiquities.

Annie Barlow was the sister of John Robert Barlow of the spinning firm Barlow & Jones, which owned some of the largest mills in Bolton from 1900, including Albert Mills, Cobden Mill and Egyptian West Mill.[5] She became involved both in the Egypt Exploration Fund and in the Chadwick Museum. In 1887, she took the opportunity to become the Local Honorary Secretary of the EEF for the Bolton area. Coming as she did, from a wealthy textile background, she was in a very good position to tap those of similar wealth for subscriptions to the EEF.

Annie Barlow visited Egypt with her brother John Robert, who was travelling to Alexandria, on business in 1888. They travelled through the Delta by train, boat and donkey, visiting several major sites including Tell Basta, Tanis and Naukratis. On her return she was able to report on her visit, to the AGM of the Egypt Exploration Fund and later to write a number of articles on the Fund's work in the Delta.

The Bolton area, with or without Annie's help, also subscribed to the Egyptian Research Account and later to the British School of Archaeology in Egypt. This backing

Fig. 26 Annie Barlow c. 1920

[4] Thomas, Angela
[5] Longworth, James H.,1987 p. 39

35

Fig. 27 One of Annie Barlow's teaching cards

for Petrie's work meant that the Chadwick Museum itself benefitted. Much of Annie's fundraising took place before the First World War, but she dedicated herself to lifelong support for Egyptological causes. As a major donor, she was entitled to a share of the proceeds from any excavation, but she chose to cede this right directly to the museum. She certainly saw a lot of Petrie in the early days and she must have given him some money. She was given a cartonnage coffin, a mummy case from Ilahun and a child's mummy, as a personal gift, but such items were too big to house, so they were given to the museum. Some of the best items, such as stones from Bubastis and a collection of coffins came from the same source. One of the major features of the collection is a group of objects from the EEF's excavations at Tell el Amarna, the site of the city of Akhetaten, built as a capital by Pharaoh Akhenaten, who had broken away from traditional Egyptian religion. The fact that much of Bolton's collection derives directly from excavations, rather than from purchases from dealers in antiquities, is fairly unusual, since many local museums were given small donations by collectors who had often bought the items. Annie Barlow devoted herself to furthering interest in Egyptology and, unsurprisingly given her background, was particularly interested in the textiles. The cards she used for teaching contained samples of ancient textiles with matching notes.

Some of these still exist today. Despite severe arthritic pain in later life, she was active in the local community and entertained Mahatma Gandhi when he visited the north of England to study the plight of the textile workers who were being adversely affected by the Indian ban on English textiles which he had been backing. Some remarkable photographs exist in the archive of the Bolton News showing a formidable-looking Annie, in a large

flower- decorated hat, walking with the dhoti-clad Gandhi in the garden of her house at Greenthorne in Edgworth in September 1931. Despite their apparent amity, it is said that they had little in common and Gandhi did not stay the night at Annie's house as was commonly believed.[6] Mrs Prifti who was there at the time told Angela Thomas that Gandhi sat on the floor to eat while his hostess and her friend had to stand.

When Annie Barlow died in 1941, the remainder of her private collection came into the Bolton Museum. The Chadwick Museum's first curator was William Waller Midgley, he and his son Thomas, who spent the whole of his working life in the Bolton Museum Service, looked after the collection for many decades. William took a big drop in salary to take the curator's job, his particular interests were natural history, textiles and the local textile industry's history. It was no big step for him to become fascinated by Egyptian textiles, of which the museum had one of the best collections in the world. The first Egyptian items arrived in 1884 from the EEF excavations at Tanis, presumably as a result of a private subscription. In a cotton town like Bolton, Egyptian textiles were held in great respect since even samples from antiquity were of the highest quality and provided inspiration for modern weavers who were able to study them. Not only are the samples beautiful but they are mostly from known contexts, which gives them particular significance for researchers.[7] Most of the best preserved samples are Coptic and date to around 300AD but the oldest fragment of linen is 5000 years old. It may well be that Midgley discussed the subject of Egyptian textiles with the man who had excavated large quantities,

---

[6] Website :Bolton News
[7].Website:Bolton Museums

36

Fig. 28 William Waller Midgley

since there is an expenses claim in the archive for Midgley's train fare to Manchester, in order to meet Petrie, who must have been giving one of his regular lectures. In 1899 Petrie gave a lecture in Bolton itself. Most of William Midgley's active work on ancient textiles was carried out after he retired in 1906, when he examined textiles from Meidum and predynastic material from Giza, as well as early dynastic period samples from Tarkhan.

Midgley's published records show that, in the tradition of the locality, his methods of study were entirely scientific and allowed him to identify the nature of the fabric and the methods used in production of the textile. His pioneering work was as important as that being carried out in the Manchester University. He built up a reputation which ensured that anything in bad condition was sent to him for some attempt at conservation. Without modern methods however, he did not always succeed, as, for example, a basket from the Fayoum, sent by the well-respected archaeologist Gertrude Caton Thompson, could not be consolidated.   He also did some work with the textiles in the collection of the Bankfield Museum in Halifax. He was not only interested in Egyptology but wrote articles on a variety of other topics, one such being on the bacilli of typhoid fever and another on humidity in cotton spinning. William passed on his expertise to his son Thomas, who continued to specialise in Egyptian textiles during his own curatorship, which lasted until 1934. The international reputation built by the Midgleys led excavators to tap their expertise and in return, the Chadwick Museum gained more examples for the collection.[8]

The special relationship between Egypt and Bolton was crowned on the 20th July 1927, when the King of Egypt honoured the town with a visit. On the occasion of Mr William Howarth's visit to Cairo, presumably in the line of business, he had invited the King to attend the celebrations commemorating the centenary of Samuel Crompton's birth on June 6th 1927. King Fuad, having been briefed about the importance of Crompton's contribution to the cotton industry, apparently expressed a wish to do so. However,

when the invitation was formally extended, his answer, relayed by his Grand Chamberlain, was that despite his desire to 'attend in person the celebrations of the centenary of one whose invention proved to be of such inestimable benefit to the cotton industry' he 'deeply regrets not being able to attend.' The letter continues, 'owing, however to the fact that Bolton is the most important centre for the spinning of Egyptian cotton, my August Sovereign will be glad to avail himself of your kind invitation to visit your town during his stay in England.' In the Bolton Evening News, on the eve of the visit, a leader appeared, praising the King as, 'a representative of the highest cultural ideals and of a notable humanism. Bolton will therefore be giving welcome to a Sovereign of conspicuously modern outlook, wide interests and keen progressive spirit.' The article concludes, 'His Majesty's visit links a modern western textile centre to the fascinating land of the Nile. He comes from the land of the Pyramids and the Sphinx, of the Pharaohs and Tutankhamen. When he sees the yarn being spun and cloth woven in Halliwell, he will be only a mile from the museum which houses yarn spun and cloth woven in Egypt 4500 years ago. Remembrance of that fact should save us from vainglorious boasting in the proper pride of showing King Fuad what Bolton does with the cotton it receives from Egypt.'

The address by the Mayor, signed by Thomas Flitcroft, Mayor, and Samuel Parker, Town Clerk, and which is preserved in the town's library reveals the pride of the Boltonian authorities in their industry. 'We offer our tribute of gratification for the generous contribution shewn by Your Majesty in honouring the town by your visit, and for the kindly interest manifested by you in our cotton spinning industry. It affords us much pleasure that Your Majesty's visit should follow so soon after the town had honoured the memory of one of her most notable sons - Samuel Crompton - whose invention of the machine known as the Spinning Mule revolutionised the spinning of cotton, consequently the manufacture of cotton goods and which in a large measure has resulted in a great and mutually satisfactory trade in cotton being developed between the town and the country of which you are the exalted head. We desire to assure your Majesty that your visit to this town around which the trade in Egyptian yarn revolves is a source of pride and satisfaction to us.'[9]

Thomas Midgley took over the role of curator at a time when the cotton industry was booming and continued the work of his father. He worked on a range of samples from about 4500BC from Karanis in the Fayoum, up to examples from the Graeco-Roman period. He was allowed to choose samples for Bolton and was able to acquire 300 of the best. Textiles from Karanis are only to be found in Bolton and Michigan, which took the rest of the material. Thomas was also a member of the Committee of the Manchester Egypt and Oriental Society the membership of which also included John Robert Barlow whose death is reported in their proceedings. Thomas retired in 1934.

---

[8] Thomas, Angela

[9] Documents relating to the visit of King Fuad to Bolton,1927 Mss

Rochdale, another major textile town, also has some fine Egyptian material. Its collection of about 2000 artefacts was largely donated by two representatives of one of the most influential local families, the Heapes. The family had businesses connected with textiles that included interests in calico printing as well as the production of cloth. The proximity of Rochdale to the Yorkshire textile towns meant that their interests were inclined towards wool rather than cotton, so their perspective was very much Rochdale based, rather than having any involvement with cotton-focussed Manchester. They did however, belong to the same kind of radical, liberal non-conformity as many other textile magnates and could claim personal friendship with men like John Bright who was a local MP.

Charles and Joseph Robert Heape were the brothers who became interested in Egyptology and gained the appreciation of their fellow townspeople by their generosity to the community. They were the sons of Samuel and Selina who spent some years in Australia building up a thriving business trading merino wool. Samuel died there in 1857, leaving his widow to travel back to Lancashire with her two sons.[10]

Once re-established, this branch of the family became deeply involved in local affairs. They were pillars of the Brimrod United Methodist Church and took a great interest in local schools. J.R. Heape was well-known and respected for his public service and in later life as Alderman Heape JP, was awarded the freedom of Rochdale, he donated much of the town's impressive art collection. His brother Charles was less active in the public sphere, partly because of his poor health, which necessitated regular visits to warmer climes. His travels in Egypt and the Holy Land were partly motivated by religious interests but resulted in a deep and scholarly knowledge of the cultures he found there. He became a personal friend of Petrie and visited his sites in Egypt. He also brought him to visit Rochdale. His brother Joseph Robert, though much busier at home, was also, according to his obituary in the Rochdale Observer in 1933, 'deeply interested in the work of excavation in Egypt and enjoyed the personal friendship of that great Egyptologist, Sir Flinders Petrie. It was to this friendship that the Rochdale Museum owes its fine Egyptian collection which has been presented by Sir Flinders through Alderman Heape and Mr Charles Heape.'[11] A large ethnographic collection donated by the Heapes was later transferred to the Manchester Museum.

The building, now the Touchstones Centre, which originally accommodated a free public library, was extended in 1903 to contain the Museum Collection. The local newspapers were full of pride in their acquisitions and they also showed a suitable respect for their excavator. One article describes not only the items, but gives a brief history of Egypt as well. It says there are a large number of pre-dynastic artefacts, found by Petrie in burials at Koptos. The paper comments that 'additional interest attaches to

the actual specimens in the Rochdale Museum, since they came from the first excavation which had ever been scientifically made of the graves of these people.'

---

[10] Heape, Charles and Heape, Richard 1904.
[11] Rochdale Observer, 1933

8. Scientific Egyptology

According to a volume of 'Manchester Faces and Places' published in 1897, 'the city is regarded by many, chiefly of those who are ill-informed as to its intellectual life and activity, as a place wholly devoted to the extension of commerce, and the citizens as being little regardful of those higher pursuits which alone can confer dignity and honour upon a community; but it is easy to prove, that on the contrary, Manchester, throughout its rapid development as a commercial city had given attention to every phase of intellectual progress and many of her citizens have made valuable contributions to the sum of scientific knowledge.'[1]

The author then goes on to cite the career of Dr Schunck, whose research provides an early example of the involvement of non-Egyptologists in the study of artefacts in the Manchester Collection. Not surprisingly, this relates to the study of textiles, since the industry was always interested in furthering its knowledge in order to incorporate it into current methods. Dr Schunck, a respected university chemist, specialised in the study of dyes. His family background in calico printing had led him to concentrate on the effects of different kinds of dye on cotton, leading him to investigate the dyestuffs used in ancient Egypt. The regard in which he was held led to a building on the university campus being named 'The Schunck Building'. His early career managing a factory near Rochdale which specialised in fulling, dyeing and bleaching gave him a lifelong interest in the chemistry of dyestuffs. He was a pioneer in the investigation of the chemical components of colours such as indigo and the purple colour from shellfish. The textiles discovered in Egypt were so well preserved that the chemistry of the dyes used could be studied.[2] This was quite in accordance with Schunck's interests and expertise.

The correspondence between Petrie and R D Darbishire of the Whitworth Institute deals in part with research that is to be carried out on these dyestuffs. Petrie had discovered many fabrics, mainly from the Coptic period, which had been dyed in various colours, Mr Darbishire's letter says, 'it appears that some of the colours on these linens are a wealth of special interest to one of our chief chemists here, and he begs me to enquire whether he could obtain for the purpose of analysis, some specimens of linen dyed red, purple, green, yellow or blue. I do not think of anyone more likely than yourself to have access to such fragments. A few square inches of a colour would be enough for research. I trust you will excuse my writing to ask whether you could send a few such 'patterns'. Dr Schunck's purpose is purely scientific. He has made a

special private study of the chemistry of vegetable dyes.'[3] The misunderstanding about exactly what samples were required which followed was, as has been shown earlier, eventually resolved.

From further letters exchanged by Petrie and Darbishire, it is clear that other researchers were keen to get their hands on samples. Petrie wrote, 'I was informed that you needed pieces for analysis and Dr Schunck said that a few square inches of each colour would suffice. But it now seems that a much larger amount is desired. I shall be glad therefore to have your list of the pieces as I suppose you have more material than is needed for analysis, perhaps you would send a small sample of each colour to Dr A. Wiederman who is desiring to examine the colours himself and had made a similar application to that I received from you.'[4]

Evidently Petrie was still a little disgruntled, since he wrote to Dr Schunck himself in 1892, pointing out that all the fragments were from Illahun and taken from Petrie's own collection by Mr Darbishire. He goes on to question some of Schunck's conclusions that had been published in the Report of the Manchester Literary and Philosophical Society, saying that they were based on imprecise information. The samples were from clothed bodies in shallow graves with no coffins. The dryness of the air had dessicated the bodies so that there was little contact with any bodily fluids. This would of necessity have affected chemical analysis. It is to be wondered how Petrie had time to keep such a close eye on every aspect of his discoveries.[5]

There are many remarkable examples of textiles from Egypt in the various collections in Greater Manchester. The Whitworth Art Gallery has a fine collection of textiles from Petrie's excavations. Many of these date from the post Pharaonic period, when Coptic Christianity was the main cultural influence. The collection includes several complete garments.

Meanwhile in Bolton, the major centre of textile manufacturing and finishing, William Midgely was perfecting his scientific methods. He published a report in 1911 which was the first of its kind on the subject of Egyptian textiles. In it he demonstrated his scientific and meticulous approach to their study. He employed the kind of method which would be used to study a modern textile, counting the number of warp and weft threads to the linear inch, the diameter of fibres, whether threads were double or single and how they were twisted. In addition, he made

---

[1] Manchester Faces and places
[2] www.chriscooksey.demon.co.uk
[3] Petrie correspondence
[4] Petrie correspondence
[5] Petrie correspondence

microscope slides and made an assessment of the condition of the sample. The first pieces to be studied in this way came from sites dating to the third and fourth dynasties and were all of linen. The next group came from pre-dynastic sites and Midgley believed they were not made from linen but from a fibre known as ramie which comes from a plant in the nettle family. This has been disputed by later scholars but the argument remains unproven. The photographic micro-slides he made are still as useful as they were in his own day. His last published work was a study of Coptic textiles which came from early dynastic contexts at Tarkhan and Kafr Ammar for Petrie himself, in 1915. When he retired he passed over his mantle to his son, Thomas who worked closely with a new generation of excavators. He carried out extensive studies on the textiles found by Guy Brunton. Much of this material was pre-dynastic and Badarian and represented the earliest samples studied to date. He made detailed studies, often using very fragile pieces and much of his work was ground-breaking. In the 1920s he was asked by an American team to study four thousand textiles from Karanis of the Graeco-Roman period. This shows in what esteem he was held, not just in Britain, but worldwide. He retired in 1934.[6]

The first major multi-disciplinary mummy study, which helped to provide the inspiration for much later and even more remarkable work, was carried out in Manchester by a notable woman. This was Margaret Murray who was to become a leading Egyptologist and academic, she had been one of Petrie's most brilliant scholars at University College London, becoming the first female full-time Egyptologist and in 1898, the first female lecturer in the subject. She was a remarkable woman who might have been lost to Egyptology had she stayed in India where she was born. There, she had been a nurse but was unable to continue this career in England as her tiny stature was thought not to be sufficiently robust for the work. Instead, her academic career spanned many decades as she lived to be a hundred years old. Margaret Drower,[7] the biographer of Petrie remembers her very well. 'Petrie didn't lecture that much, Margaret Murray did most of them. She was a very good teacher and taught many, many archaeologists. She also ran Hieroglyph and Coptic classes.' These must have been very useful to Drower when she was digging in Egypt as she recalls that she found so many Coptic ostraka that she was almost overwhelmed.

Petrie seconded Margaret Murray to Manchester in 1906 to catalogue the Haworth Collection. There she gave a well-received series of lectures and in 1908 she embarked upon the project to study the grave assemblage of the Two Brothers from Rifeh. This remarkable, untouched tomb had been found by Petrie in 1907, following earlier investigation of the area by Frank Griffith. It consists of the coffins, funerary goods of high quality, and the physical remains of Nekht Ankh and Khnum Nakht, recorded as brothers. Maspero, the Head of the Antiquities Service in

Fig. 29 Margaret Murray

Egypt had allowed the whole collection to be exported and it was given intact to the Manchester Museum. Margaret Drower comments, 'Petrie presented it to the Manchester Museum where it has pride of place in the collection - even the British Museum has no comparable tomb group.'

The arrival of this collection was recorded in the Museum Committee Report for 1907-08, 'the mummy unwrapping, investigations and forthcoming publication all being paid for out of the donations raised by appeal'. It was noted that due to the aid from Mr. Haworth, Miss Margaret Murray was able to continue with the cataloguing of the collection with the additional help of Miss Margaret Hart-Davis.[8]

The unwrapping and study of the remains of the Two Brothers was pioneering work, but although Murray published a monograph on the study and subsequently spoke to the Manchester Literary and Philosophical Society, her autobiography, 'My First Hundred Years'[9] curiously makes no mention at all of Manchester or the work she carried out there. The actual steps by which the autopsies of the two mummies were prepared and the processes of study were, sadly, not fully recorded either, although Murray did record the outcome in her monograph of 1910. The event was recorded in the press as something that would have appealed to the public imagination.

'The ceremony took place in the Chemical Theatre of the University, Miss Margaret Murray conducting the proceedings with the assistance in the unrolling of Mr Standen, Mr Wilfred Jackson, Miss Wilkinson and Miss Hart-Davis. The unrolling was witnessed by five hundred people and lasted one hour and a half. At the close of the ceremony, members of the audience who wished to have a piece of the mummy wrappings were invited by

[6] Thomas, Angela
[7] Drower, Margaret
[8] David, Rosalie 2007
[9] Murray, A. Margaret 1963

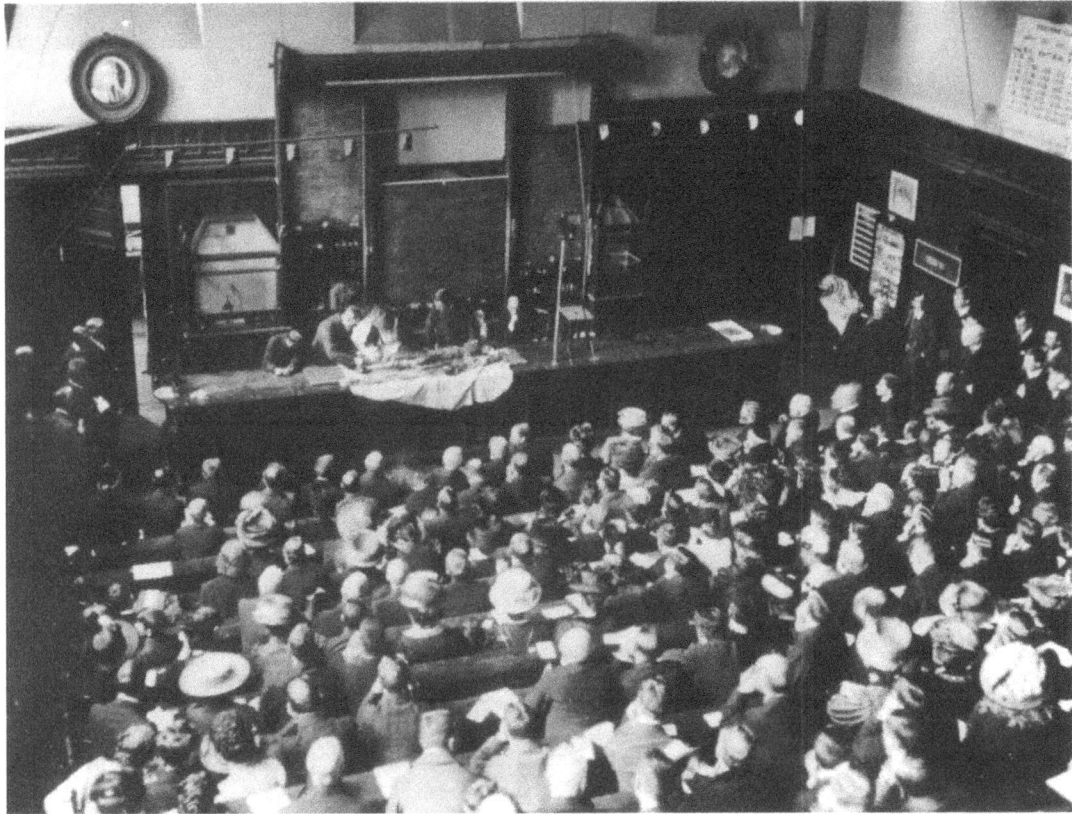

Fig. 30 The unwrapping of the two brothers

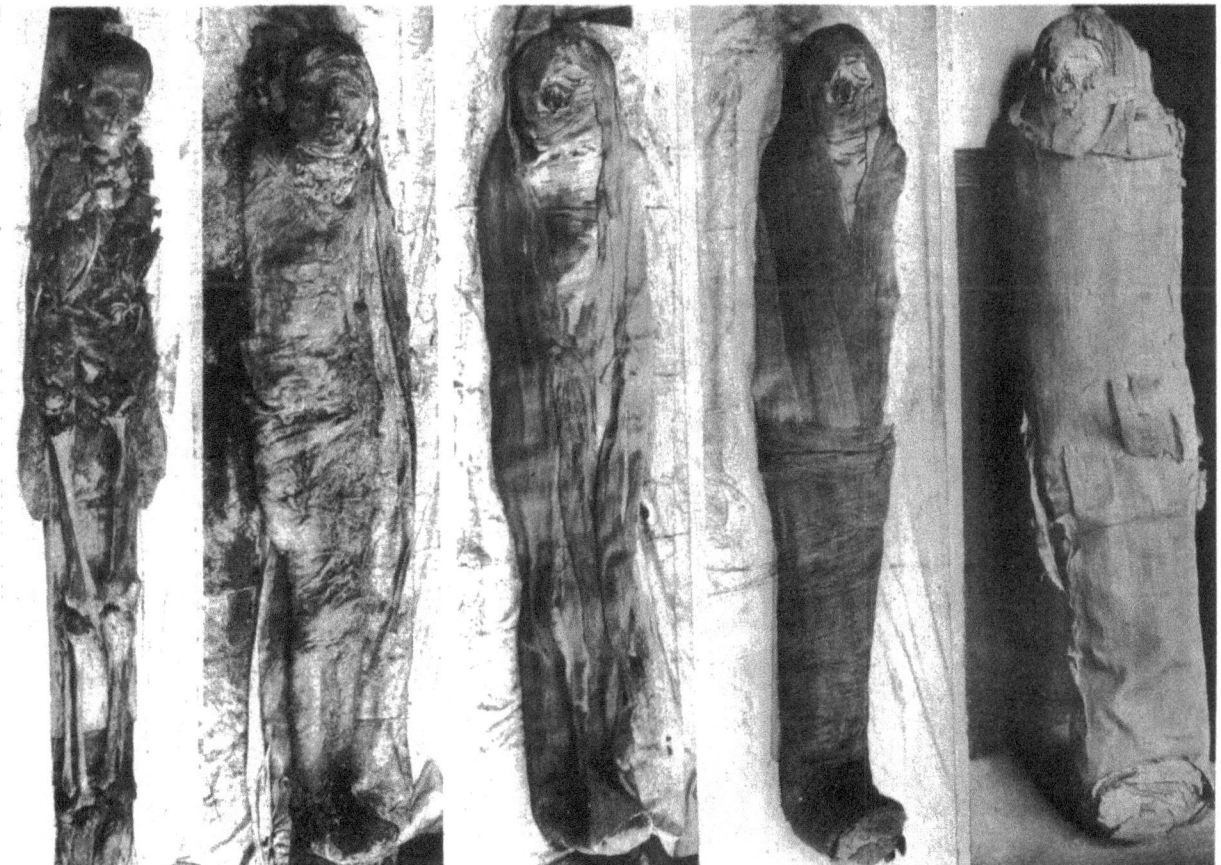

Fig. 31 Stages in unwrapping the mummies

the Chairman of the Meeting to leave their names and addresses.'[10]

The mummy wrappings were carefully studied, presumably before being distributed to the public. Specialists identified the quality and type of textile, as well as the dyestuffs used, together with the inscriptions on them. Mr. Hubner of the Municipal School of Technology was reported in the Manchester Guardian in May 1909 as having given a paper to the Society of Dyers and Colourists on the examination of no less than ninety fragments which were studied and they were all found to have been made from flax. Some were undyed, but most were dyed in light and dark yellow colours, the dye was made from safflower with the addition of certain salts. The speaker paid tribute to the work of the late Dr Schunck who, he said, had identified a range of colours in much later fabrics from Egypt.

The mummified remains were subjected to scrutiny and described in detail. Dr John Cameron, a medical expert, studied the skeletal remains, the dentition and the viscera from the canopic jars.[11] All this work was hampered by the limited means of study available to the team, in the absence of technological equipment the whole process had to be carried out by eye and the application of experience. The same material became the subject of a much more technically advanced study in the 1970s with the development of the Manchester Mummy Project directed by Rosalie David. This work, involving state of the art radiological and other equipment, was able to both build upon and correct the findings of the original Margaret Murray study. Thus began the tradition of research into paleopathology which continues to this day A notable paleopathologist with a strong Manchester connection who made a significant contribution to Egyptology was Sir Grafton Elliot Smith. Of Australian origin, he spent most of his professional life in universities, starting in Cairo in 1900. He was Professor of Anatomy in the Manchester Medical School from 1909 - 1919. In 1902 he became an expert on the human brain using material from El Amrah. He was the first scientific expert to examine the Royal Mummies in Cairo and he developed a paleopathological tradition. He was presented with a great opportunity when the first 'low' dam was being built in Nubia between 1899 and 1902. The Archaeological Survey of Nubia which was led by George Reisner produced a vast amount of material including an unrivalled collection of human remains. Elliot Smith, assisted by Frederick Wood who was also at one time connected with Manchester University, was asked to advise the survey. He was able to examine 20,000 human and animal remains providing an unrivalled opportunity to study the epidemiology of the various populations of the area, spanning the whole range of Egyptian history from pre-dynastic times on. The material collected was dispersed later to locations in Australia, America and Britain besides some being retained in Cairo. Part of the British portion found its way to Manchester where it remains. Amazingly

this unique collection has never been properly recorded or studied since Elliot Smith's day and has suffered neglect over the years.[12]

Now it is in the KNH Centre for Biomedical Egyptology in the Faculty of Life Sciences in the University and is about to become the subject of a major new research project funded by the Wellcome Trust, in partnership with the National Research Centre in Cairo, the Natural History Museum in London and the Duckworth Collection in Cambridge.

---

[12] David, Rosalie, lecture, 2010

Fig.32 A student in the KNH centre with one of the Elliot Smith collection of skulls.

---

[10] Manchester Guardian
[11] David, Rosalie 2007

9. A life devoted to Manchester Egyptology

Fig 33 A rare photo of Winifred Crompton

An important arrival at the Museum in the first decade of the twentieth century was Winifred Crompton, who was to make a significant contribution to its development over nearly thirty years. She was appointed in 1905 to replace Miss Standen as official printer of labels. This rather humble, though important post, was only a beginning, since in 1912 she was appointed Assistant to take charge of Egyptology and Anthropology. Miss Crompton was born in Old Trafford in 1870. Her father was a pharmaceutical chemist and she was privileged enough to study at Manchester University. She was actively involved with the planning of the layout of the new Haworth wing of the Museum, a project on which she worked closely with Petrie. She became a personal friend of the Petries and visited them on site in Egypt.

Over the following years she worked tirelessly to promote the cause of Egyptology, she earned an honorary MA from the University for her work both in the Egyptology Department of the Museum and in teaching the subject to successive generations of schoolchildren. Her premature death in 1932 on a tramcar outside the Royal Infirmary on her way to work must have been a great shock to her colleagues and was certainly a great loss to the cause of Egyptology in Manchester. The impression given by the tributes paid to her after her death suggests a keen mind, a dedication to hard work and enormous enthusiasm. Dr G.H. Carpenter delivered a warm commendation at her funeral. 'The museum collections as they stand today are a memorial of a wide and accurate knowledge, her untiring industry, her skill in handicraft, her cultivated taste, her sound judgement and her zeal in passing on to others 'the good treasure' of her mind.'[1] Sir Grafton Elliot Smith summarised her qualities in the Annual Report of the Manchester Egyptian and Oriental Society for 1932-33. 'Miss Crompton took a keen personal pride in the Egyptian objects in the Museum, and by immense devotion acquired an exact knowledge and critical estimate not merely of them, but also of the whole field of Egyptian history and archaeology. She was always ready generously and unselfishly to place this knowledge at the service of anyone who needed it and even to undertake investigations for others.' He concluded by saying that her life 'was devoted heart and soul to the promotion of Egyptology in Manchester.'[2] In her approach to her work she was providing a model for future generations.

She was a scholar with a sharp, critical mind, an enterprising researcher, and, above all an enthusiastic communicator. Her ability to interpret the objects in her care and to interest people in them was in 'a large measure responsible for promoting the cultivation of Egyptian studies in the Museum and the University'[3] A further description of her contribution was presented by Dr Canney in the same journal. He pointed out that the association between the Museum and the University had always been of mutual advantage. Miss Crompton was able to gain maximum value from this by attending all the lecture courses given over the years by leading Egyptologists at the University. notably F. Llewellyn Griffith until 1908, Alan H. Gardiner between 1912 and 1914 and T. Eric Peet who followed. She also attended all the lectures given by Petrie himself. This gave her a real mastery over the subject.[4] So today, in the twenty first century, the work done over the last forty years in the Museum and its continuance in the KNH Centre

[1] Carpenter, G.H ,in Manchester Egyptian and Oriental Society Report for 1932-33
[2] G. Elliot Smith in Manchester Egyptian and Oriental Society Report for 1932-33
[3] G. Elliot Smith in Manchester Egyptian and Oriental Society for 1932-33
[4] Canney in Manchester Egyptian and Oriental Society for 1932-33

at the University follows in this tradition of promoting knowledge and firing enthusiasm for the subject.

Miss Crompton's first major job was to complete the labels for the Two Brothers collection and in 1909 she supplied a complete list of the tomb furniture to Margaret Murray who needed it for her book on the subject. In 1910 she seems to have had a very busy year as the Committee reported that 'conservation was required on the inscribed Egyptian stone slabs which had deteriorated due to the damp, acid-laden Manchester atmosphere and also re-identification of these objects was carried out by Miss W. Crompton together with proof correction for the new handbook of Egyptian Antiquities to be published.' In March 1911 she was holding a demonstration one evening on 'Ancient Egyptian Implements'. This was one of many Wednesday evening sessions over the next few months on a range of Egyptian topics. At the same time she was working hard to transfer the Egyptian collections to their new home in the Haworth Building. A hint that the effects of the cotton industry were not necessarily always beneficial is given, when in 1912 she refused the offer of a sculpture from Petrie's excavation of the labyrinth at Hawara 'owing to the difficulty of preserving limestone in Manchester.' Presumably the damp climate and the pollution were the reasons for her concern.

The arrangement of the Egyptian Collection and its updated catalogue must have occupied a good deal of her time over the next few years. She was said to have been 'happy in the opportunity of setting out the objects that she loved to a greater advantage even than before.'[5]

In the museum store there are some small Egyptian items with a note in Miss Crompton's hand. It reads 'Found slightly mouldy and dried before the fire. Brushed with methylated spirits. 1917. WMC'. During this time she was in correspondence with Petrie about many things, including the acquisition of new material for the Museum. In 1913 Petrie wrote in a rather jocular fashion, 'the enclosed lists will show you how far your covetousness has been rewarded'. Apparently they had had to pay nearly £2 per scarab to Cairo Museum 'to ransom them'.

Just before the outbreak of the First World War, Jesse Haworth donated a magnificent pectoral of cloisonné work and its associated ornaments dating to the XIIth Dynasty, which he had bought from Petrie who had found it in the previous digging season. Haworth was taking an active interest in the work of Miss Crompton. In 1913 he wrote to her about the textiles cleaned and mounted by the late Kate Bradbury Griffith. He would have liked to retain the original mounts but accepted that now they were in the Museum they would need to be displayed in a suitable fashion. He bore the cost of this work. Two years later, Haworth wrote to Miss Crompton to thank her for 'the beautiful illuminated address which came as a great

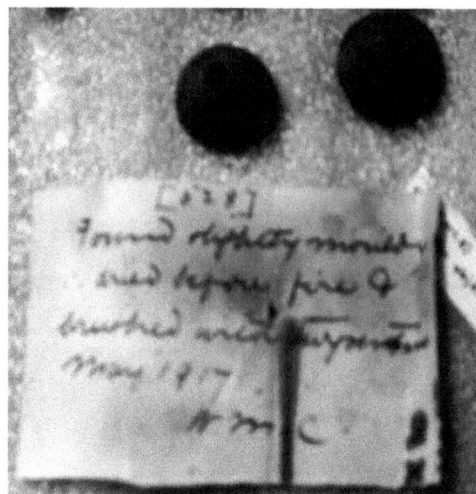

Fig. 34 Miss Crompton's work

surprise.' This was to mark his 80th birthday and he was sure she must have had a hand in it.

The Great War interrupted the reporting of work at the museum but new opportunities to offer educational facilities were taken up. Miss Crompton began running four classes for schoolchildren each week. Around 900 to 1000 were able to benefit. In 1915 this was said to be in the experimental stage but it was hoped to build a permanent link with elementary education in Manchester. In the same year Miss Crompton was busy restoring and mounting Coptic cloths and embroideries and preparing labels for Haworth's latest donations. She was also writing articles for various publications. In the JEA, published in 1916, she described two clay balls in the Manchester Collection which contained tufts of human hair. In the annual report of the Manchester Egypt and Oriental Society in the same year she presented a tribute to the great Egyptologist Gaston Maspero who had died in the previous year.

The following year, since British activities in Egypt had been suspended because of the war, she occupied herself classifying and arranging the collections of scarabs and seals. In 1917 she was sorting out problems caused by damp in the store rooms. The committee, perhaps hoping for some funding, noted that 'dry and roomy storerooms are particularly necessary if the reserve collections are to be properly cared for.' Winifred was in correspondence with leading experts of the day like Sir Alan Gardiner who wrote to her explaining a scarab inscription .

Miss Crompton seems to have been very modest about her talents and apparently disclaimed her achievements, crediting her predecessors with the current state of the museum. Hilda Petrie wrote to her in 1915 suggesting that she was too modest 'It strikes me you live on your own reputation and not in the parasitic manner you describe! I do not see that former people have more than a former share- down to the time they left it - I mean -for the neat arrangement of the Museum and they are not responsible

---

[5] Manchester Egyptian and Oriental Society for 1932-33, Funeral Report.

for the present virtues of curating. The labelling is indeed excellent.'

After the war Winifred's extensive correspondence continued. In 1920 she had been trying to find a list of the symbols which the ancient Egyptians used to identify their provinces, the Nome signs. She approached Margaret Murray for help and received an encouraging reply. 'It is better to go for the early things, and this can only be done by an Egyptologist. Why don't you work up some of these points yourself? It is time you did a piece of solid research, and this is a good subject to begin on, just go ahead and do it, you are quite qualified for it. Take the Nome signs and find out all the early signs; this will throw a flood of light on the local ceremonies and on the early religious beliefs. The John Rylands Library will get you the books you want, if they know you are really in need of them. Don't be afraid of asking and don't be afraid of tackling a subject that is quite within your powers. Yours affect. M. Murray.' In another letter Murray provided good advice for any researcher, even today, 'there is no royal road to research. You must look through everything that has been published; keep careful notes in a book, and never trust to your memory. Kept with this letter is a list of Nomes with their signs, deities, animal relics and agricultural ceremonies in Miss Crompton's own hand, suggesting that she took Miss Murray's advice. Further help was offered in 1922 when Margaret Murray passed on some tips about reading cartouches and genealogies on inscriptions. For the next eleven years she continued her busy schedule, perhaps wearing herself out in the process.

Outside her work, she had a Christian radical approach to life which was typical of so many of her fellow Mancunians. Her spare time was taken up with social service in the University Settlement and in humble town parishes. She also shared her knowledge by means of illustrated lectures and espoused the causes of world peace and human brotherhood, besides making varied efforts for the welfare of women and children.

10. Museums after World War One

Once the First World War finished, it would be supposed that the normal routines of the Museum in Manchester would have been resumed , however there seem to be no reports from the Museum Committee between 1918 and 1921.[1] When their publication restarted, the usual pattern of activity is recorded. The reports made no mention of the momentous discovery of 1922 at the time, but Winifred Crompton's correspondents were excited by it. Ironically there is a letter from Mrs Haworth in which she laments the lack of enthusiasm for Egyptian exploration amongst the younger generation.[2] Writing in 1921 she could not anticipate the events which were to change everything twelve months hence. A letter from Hilda Petrie in 1922 let Miss Crompton know that 'there had just been a tremendous find in the tombs of the Kings by Mr Carter, of XVIIIth Dynasty, furniture, time of Tutankhamen and going back to Akhenaten - a new royal tomb apparently. You will see something in today's 'Times' and other papers.'[3] This was, of course, the find of the century which created an enormous impression in the minds of the public. It also fired the enthusiasm of the Egyptological world. Margaret Murray wrote to her in April 1923 that she had been very busy lecturing and writing. 'Tut has certainly increased the interest in Egyptology to an extraordinary extent the number of lectures that are being wanted is also extraordinary.'[4]

An interesting series of letters from F. Bibby & Co, of Corporation Street in Manchester refers to a quarterly journal on Ancient Egypt and asks for a supply on trade terms, as well as a list of books on Egyptology suitable for the general reader, since he has observed a growing public interest in the subject. 'This morning for instance, the undersigned in travelling down to town found that the subject of conversation in the railway compartment was the opening of the inner chamber at Luxor and one or two gentlemen said that it was a very fascinating thing to read about but they would like to get hold of a book that would give them some light on the history of the time referred to, and also of the excavations which have been made from time to time'[5]. This illustrates how public interest had been fired by the discovery. At the Manchester Museum Harry Spencer, a veteran who had lost his leg in the war, was an invaluable member of staff. As technician, he could turn his hand to many things and was the creator of accurate models. Inspired by the discovery, he produced a model of the tomb of Tutankhamun for display in the museum which would have been a popular attraction for the public.[6]

Fig.35 Marianne Haworth, now confined in the Museum store

In 1923 a collection of fine glazed wares was acquired as well as some fine archaic objects from Petrie's excavations at Abydos. All this new material had to be housed and concern was being expressed at the lack of damp-free storage rooms and proper showcases. It was hoped that these problems would be solved by the new extension which was just beginning to be built, using Jesse Haworth's generous legacy.

Mrs Haworth continued the tradition set by her late husband. Winifred Crompton herself went to London in 1923 to select material from the Qua el Kebir excavation by the British School of Archaeology in Egypt. Artefacts continued to arrive from this source throughout the next three years. At the same time an active programme of lectures was continuing. Petrie himself delivered annual talks in these years, mainly relating to the predynastic and archaic periods. Eric Peet, who, as a lecturer at Manchester

---

[1] Fildes George , Minutes of Museum Committee, unpublished
[2] Archive Correspondence Manchester Museum
[3] Archive Correspondence Manchester Museum
[4] Archive Correspondence Manchester Museum
[5] Archive Correspondence Manchester Museum
[6] Fildes George , Minutes of Museum Committee, unpublished.

during the war had contributed to the Museum's programme of lectures, continued to do so now that he was Professor of Egyptology at Liverpool. In 1928 he presented a whole series which showed the continuing interest in relating Egyptian and Biblical history. It was entitled 'Egypt and the Old Testament' and covered the topics of Joseph, the Sojourn in Egypt and the Exodus.

In 1929 Miss Crompton was helped by a young Manchester graduate called Mary Shaw who was about to go to Oxford to study Egyptology. She was to take over Miss Crompton's position after the latter's very sudden and unexpected death in 1933.

As the new Assistant Keeper, Mary Shaw continued in the tradition set by her predecessor. She was reported in 1933 as increasing the attractiveness of the Egyptian Display. She was also responsible for overseeing conservation work on Asru's mummy cases which were cleaned and protected by a coat of unspecified preservative and displayed in an upright position. She also worked to conserve the coffin of Khary, which had recently arrived in a much decayed state. Gifts of Egyptian antiquities continued to arrive throughout the 1930s, including a share of Petrie's finds from Gaza. 1937 was a particularly good year when the Museum received a large collection of slate palettes and other items from Mrs Rutherston Powell, and another collection, of Egyptian art, came from the late Professor Speigelberg. Another active supporter of the Museum, Rollo Worthington was busy raising money for the EES excavations in the Sudan.

During the Second World War, the service provided by the Museum to the public was continued as far as possible but work had to be done to protect some of the most valuable items. School classes were still being held, though in a limited way, and a refuge was opened under the Museum in case of air raids. Mary Shaw continued to work on the collections and to lecture but she had added responsibilities since she was appointed Control Room secretary, presumably a post unconnected with Egyptology. In 1943 she was reported as having most of her time taken up with A.R.P. duties but there were still lectures and a steady, though reduced, flow of acquisitions, including some Graeco-Roman and Coptic items from Major Gayer Anderson Pasha whose house in Cairo is now a museum.

Once the war ended there was much to be done in reorganising the collection, much of which had been in store in rural Yorkshire for the duration but by 1947 things were nearly back to normal. In 1948, Mary Shaw resigned as she was about to become Mrs Palmer. Her successor, Elise Baumgartel, only stayed two years, before going to America. During her time, a new laboratory was established for the Egyptian and Classical departments.

Theodore Burton-Brown who took over as Assistant Keeper of Archaeology, remarkably the first male holder of this post after 1912, stayed for eighteen years. His interests lay in ancient Anatolia rather than Egypt so the Museum Committee Reports are less informative about

the Egyptian Collection than some of the earlier ones. One reason for this lessening of interest in the subject could be related to the political situation. The Suez Crisis of 1956 resulted in the termination of the huge link between Britain and Egypt and there were no visitors in Egypt for some time afterwards. One major acquisition, in 1959, was the Robinow Collection which was the subject of a special exhibition. Towards the end of the 1960s a new experimental approach was adopted which was to lay the foundation for the remarkable pioneering Mummy Project begun in the 1970s which preceded the work which continues today.

Meanwhile in Bolton, Thomas Midgley continued to run the Egyptian collection until his death in 1934. He would probably have been distressed to know that the Chadwick Museum closed in 1937, despite some local opposition, but the building had dry rot, so it was demolished in 1957. The Art Gallery and Museum was built to match the Town Hall but when it opened only the Natural History Collection went to the Museum. The Egyptian Collection, despite a vocal lobby of people such as local teachers, was not seen between 1937 and 1962, since it was in store. During the 1940s and 1950s, because of post war austerity museums went through a period of rationalisation since they were of a low priority. This point is illustrated by the fact that in Bolton, for example, the Curator was also the Coal Officer. Throughout these vicissitudes the Curator from 1934-1956 was Thomas Midgley's assistant Eric Hendy who was followed by Alfred Hazelwood who died in 1961 at the young age of 48. He was a natural historian interested in Egypt and he encouraged students to research but did not himself work on the Egyptian material. After his death the Egyptian Gallery was created in his memory. It allowed the collection to see the light of day again but it needed an Egyptologist to sort it out.

This task fell to Angela Thomas who was able to reorganise the collection. Her predecessor, Pauline Beswick had kept the collection in good condition, but as a British archaeologist her real interests lay elsewhere. One of Angela Thomas' first jobs was eject an alien body from the display, that of a Peruvian whose presence had been rather misleading. During her Keepership at Bolton, the Egyptian Collection was brought to life. The whole gallery had two reorganisations, each without much funding. There were a number of temporary exhibitions which allowed the Bolton Collection to be given a high profile in print and through the media. The reputation of the Museum grew and researchers and interested parties from Britain and overseas increased. Education was, as it has been in Manchester, a priority. Teaching packs and support for school projects were developed. These gained popularity when Egypt was officially included in the National Curriculum for Primary Schools in 1988. Evening classes for adults further enhanced interest in the subject and researchers were encouraged to use the artefacts in the collection. Angela Thomas retired from Bolton in 2005.[7]

7 Thomas, Angela. 2007

In 1977, the Museum was given a quantity of linen by the Petrie Museum in London but much of this requires proper study. In 1979 Stand Grammar School donated a collection of artefacts including a few Egyptian items and in 1981 the Wellcome Museum for the History of Medicine gave over 300 objects, mostly textiles. Some of these were portions of mummy wrappings, rare painted cloths and animal mummies. In this collection there are some rare specimens. These include examples of painted mummy cloths which were in a very fragile state. Many of these, including one associated with Hatshepsut, have been painstakingly restored by Jacqueline Hyman, an independent conservator. [8]

A less fortunate acquisition was also one of the most recent. The notorious case of the Bolton forgers, the Greenhalgh family, is now a matter of public record. The sculpture of an Amarna princess appeared to be a great addition to the Amarna material already in the collection and her presence encouraged new visitors. However she was revealed to have been made in a Bolton council house and her creator is, at the time of writing, serving a prison sentence. Despite the sad fact that she is not an ancient piece, there is no doubt that she is rather beautiful and perhaps deserves to be displayed, albeit under her proper identity.

The Bolton textiles are still the focus of international research interests. A well-known researcher who used some of the collection as part of her PhD research is Dr Gillian Vogelsang Eastwood who gave a talk to the Manchester Ancient Egypt Society a few years ago on the subject of Tutankhamen's wardrobe. She has said that 'the Bolton Collection of archaeological textiles is one of the most interesting yet least appreciated collections in Britain'. In the early 21st Century some of Bolton's collection, which is capable of being dated reasonably closely, because of its known provenance, is part of an international research project into Carbon 14 dating.

In Rochdale, as in Bolton, Egyptology suffered a decline after the war. The Egyptian Collection has, sadly, not been fully displayed for many years. The Second World War meant many of the valuables had to be placed in storage. For a few years, between 1974 and 1989 there was a proper museum display housed in an old rectory building but lack of funding relegated most of it to storage. Much of the storage space was unsuitable, being housed in such places as disused and damp mills. It was only in 1996 that a unit on an industrial estate was acquired, providing the opportunity to set up proper conditions for conservation. Now the whole Egyptian Collection is kept in ideal conditions in properly constructed drawers and cupboards with controlled temperature and humidity. It is available for study, but rarely put on public display. The current Collection Manager, Andrew Moore, is attempting to update the catalogue and to establish a virtual exhibition via a web-site. The last computerised record was made in the early days of computing and is stored on old-fashioned disks which can no longer be read by modern equipment. Visits to this resource centre are encouraged and material is available for use by local schools.

An exciting new initiative is planned, funding permitting, involving both the Rochdale collection and the Petrie Museum in London. It is to be called 'Time Space People: Egypt and England Ancient and Modern'. The project is aimed at linking social historical archival research and current Egyptian archaeology, in order to reveal, through small-scale public display, the multiple human lives hidden in material from the past. New fieldwork and theory continually change the interpretation of collections formed over preceding generations, while material from old excavations may remain unparalleled. If these have been properly documented, they can act as a scientific control medium for testing ideas and evaluating new finds. Finds from excavations by Flinders Petrie between 1883 and 1924 are held all over the UK and Rochdale has a substantial share. Any researcher or museum visitor today depends on forgotten groups: the excavation workforce unearthing finds in the ground, and the working-class unloading freight and constructing display. Workers in the places of display may then have visited those displays, but their participation and attitudes remain under-investigated. The Petrie Museum of Egyptian Archaeology UCL preserves, 1880s - 1920s name-lists of Egyptian diggers, and regional museums, libraries and archives hold unexplored published and unpublished papers recording the local reception of Egyptian finds. In the proposed two-year project, one researcher in late nineteenth-century social history and one in Egyptian archaeology would aim to identify the most relevant material in the archives of the Petrie Museum and northwest regional libraries and museums, and in the archaeology held in Rochdale. Rochdale Arts and Heritage Service holds one of the larger regional Egyptian archaeology collections in England from continuing annual excavation sponsorship between 1895 and 1927. Most well-documented finds in museum collections of Egyptian archaeology are from burials. Therefore the project's final display would aim to promote public debate on the ethics of displaying material where owner consent cannot be assumed; these issues arise with any archaeological material, but the debate is currently most active around human remains. If sufficient funds can be raised, the plan is to set up a single-gallery exhibition at Rochdale, acting as an opportunity for public evaluation of the project. [9]

---

[8] Hyman, Jacqueline ,2010

[9] Quirke, Stephen, 2008

Part 2

THE KNH CENTRE FOR BIOMEDICAL EGYPTOLOGY
MANCHESTER 2003

A New Era

11. New heights through new depths

The decade of the 1970s marked a watershed in the history of the Manchester Museum. Although always a centre of academic research, it reached new heights of national and international recognition with the development of a multi-disciplinary research team which would use the most modern scientific methods available, to study the materials in the Egyptian collection, particularly the human mummies. For a number of years the museum had employed no specialist Egyptologist, despite the importance of its Egyptian collection, the display of which, according to the Manchester Museum Committee Report for 1968, 'is said by foreign visitors to be amongst the best in Europe'.[1] In the following year it was reported that the Egyptian Collection was complete, apart from the writing of formal descriptive labels. The Egyptian and Classical Department had been converted into the Archaeological Department at that time and in the same year Burton - Brown retired after 18 years in post. He was succeeded by John Prag who, although his particular interest was Classical archaeology, set about some reorganisation of the reserve collection and urgent conservation was carried out on some of the mummy portraits and the coffin of Asru.

In the 1960s the museum, taking advantage of its remarkable collection, already had some interesting projects in progress. In line with what was happening elsewhere at the time, such as the work done by Harris in Cairo on the Royal Mummies, some of the Manchester mummies were X-rayed by Roy White and the staff of the Radiological Inspection Laboratories, giving some notable results despite the fairly simple nature of the portable equipment which had to be assembled in the galleries.[2] This was a precursor to much more detailed work which was able to make use of the new technological advances in the next decade. An earlier expert, Grafton Elliot Smith, Professor of Anatomy in the University of Manchester in 1909, was outstanding in his field. He had, at the time of the building of the first Aswan Dam autopsied 6,000 mummies. His large collection of skulls in Manchester provided the opportunity for studying the dental health of the ancient Egyptians. An exhibition of 'Bread and Teeth in Ancient Egypt', in co-operation with Kings College Dental Hospital, brought together Egyptian skulls and ancient teeth with samples of grain and bread. In order to analyse the evidence on display, John Prag carried out some practical experiments with saddle querns and grain in order to investigate the possible addition of grit in the grinding process which would have contributed to wear on teeth. Frank Filce Leek, who was later to make a significant contribution to the Manchester Mummy Project worked

with Sylvia Hunt and N J D Smith, two research dentists. Their research led to much publicity and the first of many television programmes.[3] It laid a foundation for the studies on human remains which were to create Manchester's international reputation.

These exciting developments highlighted the need for more specialist help in the department and it was decided to appoint a new Assistant Keeper. The appointment of Dr A. Rosalie David was made in 1972 and she took up her post on the first of June. In the report dated 31st July 1972 she is said to be 'sorting and checking the collection of scarabs'.[4] Early in the next year she had organised the replacement of the old hand-written labels and was checking the reserve collections. The notable collection of material from Kahun, excavated by Petrie and given to the Museum by Jesse Haworth, was the next area to come under her scrutiny and a detailed catalogue was projected, first in the form of a card index which would then be converted into a full catalogue arranged by type and provenance. It seems amazing that such an important collection which came to the Museum from excavations carried out in the 1890s had not yet been properly recorded, though a list had been compiled in 1910 by Miss Griffith.[5]

By the end of 1973 it had already become clear that Rosalie David was a moving spirit both inside and outside the Museum. Her research interests were developing rapidly, yet at the same time she never lost sight of her desire to disseminate knowledge and the love of Egyptology as far as possible. Her ability to communicate and to pass on her enthusiasm influenced many people in the Manchester area and beyond, and has continued to do so. In 1973 she led a party from the Extra-Mural Department of the University to Egypt. This was the first of many such visits, and a precursor to the introduction of a certificate course which has had a profound effect on many people's lives and careers. Already she was following the advice given to her by Professor Harry Smith at the Petrie Museum in London when she first got the job in Manchester, 'don't be remembered for moving the scarabs from one drawer to another.'[6]

Besides all this activity, programmes were being devised in the Museum to analyse the mummified material in the collection, a development which was to become central to the work of the department. More detailed dental X-raying was carried out by Ruth McGuiness at the Dental Hospital continuing the studies already begun. Roy Garner and

---

[1] Manchester Museum Committee Report, 1968, after Fildes
[2].David, Rosalie, 2005 interview

[3] Manchester Museum Committee Report, 1971, after Fildes
[4] Museum Committee Reports 1972, after Fildes
[5] Griffith, A. S. 1910
[6] David, Rosalie, Interview 2005

Renee Stafford meanwhile had begun to look at some of the mummified tissue in the museum.[7] Roy Garner had originally been at the North Manchester Hospital as a technician but had subsequently moved across to the Museum. He was now attached to the museum's zoology department and was experimenting on various possible methods of embalming, starting from Herodotus' account which named natron as the main chemical used to desiccate a body. Firstly he had to analyse the content of the substance. The main components were shown to be sodium carbonate and sodium bicarbonate with some added impurities including sodium chloride. He made up a solution with 65% of the true natron salts and experimented on laboratory rats and mice. A number of experiments were carried out using different methods including dry salts, a wet solution, and the injection of oil as mentioned by Herodotus, followed by submersion in dry natron. The experiments produced considerable data regarding the chemical content and amount required, the effect of the drying body on the natron, the result of exposure of the body to possible insect activity and the relative time which the process would take. Overall, the submersion in dry natron produced the best results and the sad remains of the experimental rodents were put on display in the museum.[8]

In 1973, following the earlier pioneering work of Margaret Murray, a multidisciplinary scientific team led by Rosalie David was set up. The Manchester Egyptian Mummy Research Project had as many as fifteen specialists drawn from the fields of medicine, science and Egyptology who could be called upon to share their expertise at any point in the research process. The aims of this project were initially twofold. Firstly it was intended to develop a methodology for the examination of Egyptian mummies which could be used and adapted by other researchers in the field. Secondly it was aimed at discovering specific information about disease, cause of death, diet, living conditions and funerary beliefs in ancient Egypt.[9] The protocol established allowed Manchester to become an acknowledged pioneer and leader in the field of paleopathology. In particular its development of non-destructive techniques of investigation has been accepted as the way forward by many research programmes world-wide.

The use of state of the art techniques has always been the hallmark of the Manchester Methodology. A number of factors helped this to happen. Manchester Museum, being part of the University, could draw on resources which might not be available to other museums. At that time the authorities of the University and of the Museum itself had a very 'supportive attitude.'[10] The Royal Infirmary, whose close proximity made the transportation of mummies possible, is just across the road from the Museum and is also part of the University. Furthermore, financial and practical aid came from the British Academy and from Kodak Ltd. who supplied much of the film. This meant

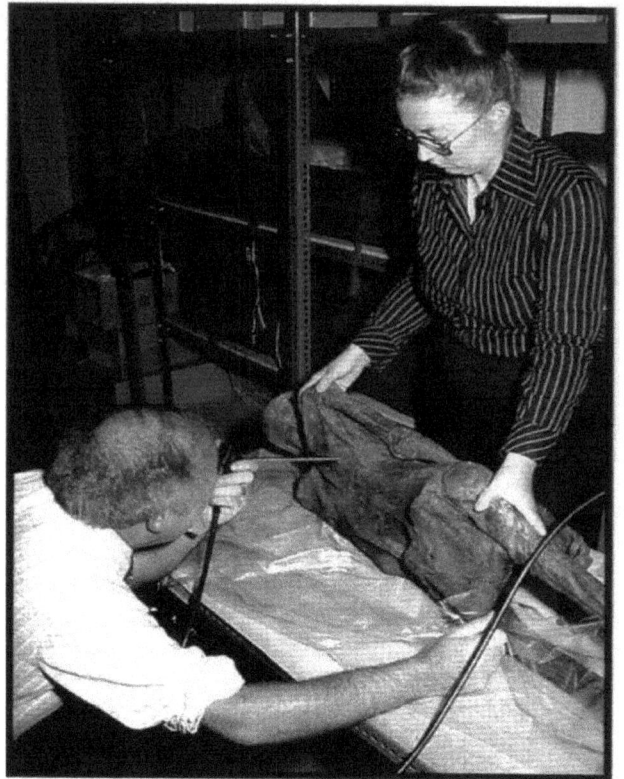

Fig. 36 Dr David studying one of the Manchester mummies

that a project to examine the mummies involving the latest techniques in radiography, scanning and endoscopy was a practical possibility and a protocol was laid down which would form the basis of future work involving other collections.

---

[7] Museum Committee Reports 1972, after Fildes
[8] Garner in ed. A. R. David, 1979
[9] ix David, Rosalie 2007
[10] David, A.R, 1979

12. Getting down to the bare bones

Rosalie David came into contact with Professor Ian Isherwood who was Consultant Radiologist at Manchester Royal Infirmary. She says he was 'the real moving spirit'. Isherwood was in charge of the Department of Neurology and had been responsible for starting a new department in the Medical School. Initially this was on a very small scale, in a single room. He became the first Professor of Radiology in 1975. From a tiny department in one room he went on to preside over many rooms and a large staff, equipped with one of the first brain scanners in the world. In 1973, before he took the chair, there were only three such brain scanners in existence, one in Glasgow, one in London, and the one in Manchester. He was interested in the early X-ray work so far carried out on the Manchester mummies but was keen to put it on a proper footing using the new equipment at his disposal. The earlier work on X-raying mummies had not involved moving any of the mummies to another location; any study which had been done took place in the Museum and was, of necessity, rather limited. Plates could not be processed on site and the researcher did not know whether the result was satisfactory. When Dr David decided that it was time to set up a new multi-disciplinary team which could make use of all this latest technology there were development grants forthcoming from the Medical Research Council, the Regional Authority and the Wellcome Trust. According to Isherwood it was a question of being in the right place at the right time and with access to state of the art equipment.[1]

At that time there were seventeen human mummies in the collection which covered between them nearly two thousand years of Egyptian history, from the twelfth dynasty to the Roman period, so they could provide information on a broad spectrum of topics. Under Isherwood's guidance these mummies were taken out of the Museum to the Infirmary at weekends when there were few patients around. It could have been rather a shock to any who were there to see patients in such a poor state of health. Using modern techniques it was hoped to gain new insights into health, ages at death, the presence of parasites and aspects of funerary practice.

As Isherwood explained 'We could determine how the body was positioned inside the cartonnage. We could X-ray and put on markers to show where the body actually lay. We had a dark room next door so could process the plates immediately and do them again if we needed. We had equipment which was of its time very advanced, you could picture the head say, and move the equipment all round the sphere to take photographs which came up on a TV screen. Then you could take tomograms which are

slices through. The slices were very thick -2cm at that time. If you take a tomogram you can blur out parts to see what lies behind, so an individual's arms, folded over the abdomen can be blurred out to reveal the spine. Computed tomography works on a different principle - it passes X-rays through and can take one slice at a time without the use of the blurring technique, 30 years on, slices of less than 1mm can be taken. Nowadays you can reconstruct the whole thing on any plane, which was not easy to do in the early days.'[2]

Several of the mummies studied in this way revealed, through study of the teeth and the stages of fusion of the bones, an early age of death and, in some cases, evidence of poor health in childhood, shown by the presence of Harris lines of arrested growth in the long bones. The results of these studies were recorded using a particular system. This led to the establishment of the Egyptian Collection Data Bank which was eventually recorded on computer. At that time these techniques were right up to date. As technology has advanced, and especially with the increasing sophistication of computers, the Manchester Project has continued to move with the times so that the most advanced available methods are always employed.

Another pioneering area of research was the development of paleopathology, that is, the use of pathological techniques to study ancient human tissue. A leading role in this was played by a well-respected local pathologist. When Rosalie David was getting people together to work on the mummified tissue, she was looking for someone to do the histology. She asked Roy Garner who was already working with her but he said that he did not have the equipment or the facilities. He did, however, know a man who had both, whom he was prepared to approach. This was the Consultant Pathologist at South Manchester Hospital, Eddie Tapp who said, 'you're probably wasting your time but I'll have a go.'[3] At that time he had no background in Egyptology but, like many others he became an enthusiast. This was the start of a notable collaboration which caught the public imagination as well as furthering knowledge of ancient Egypt and establishing new methods which would set the pattern for many years to come.

According to Tapp they began on some hands and feet which were in the store somewhere and he took some small pieces. He emphasises that he had a great deal of help from his technicians in the pathology laboratories who became very interested and who prepared some very good histological slides. He was quite surprised at the result which was more productive than he had expected.

[1] Isherwood, Ian, 2007

[2] Isherwood, Ian, 2007
[3] Tapp, Eddie, 2008

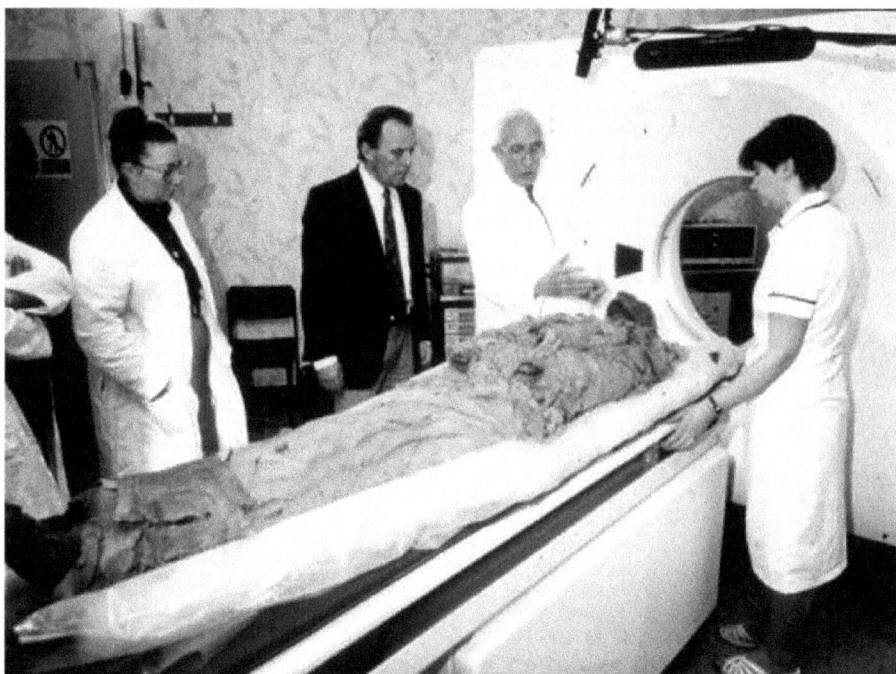

Fig.37 Professor Isherwood supervises the scanning of a mummy watched by Rosalie David.

They also experimented with different ways of rehydrating and fixing the tissue. Dr Tapp, although a very busy man in his own field, continued to work on the human remains in Manchester Museum, as well as many from other sources. Tapp's description of the work he carried out at that time illustrates vividly the way in which the studies done by the Manchester team both made use of known techniques and experimented with new ones. This was the first of many ground-breaking studies. They were following in the footsteps of the eminent anatomist, who was working early in the twentieth century, Armand Ruffer, but he 'was really the only person prior to this work who had studied soft tissue -others had looked at bones, but not tissue - so we were the first after Ruffer. Very few people spent any time on this, the only other person who had, was Sandison from Glasgow.' Since this was a whole new area of research, the methods used had to be adapted when studying ancient, rather than modern, tissue samples. 'We experimented on different ways of re-hydrating tissue - you've got to be experimental. If you have a routine biopsy of a sample in a hospital, you follow a procedure - you fix it in formaldehyde, embed it in wax and cut sections and stain each section and study it - nice and easy, but with mummy tissue you have to re-hydrate it in the first place, then you have to decide how to fix it because once it's been re-hydrated, it starts going bad, starts decomposing. The only reason mummies don't decompose is because the water has been taken out and the enzymes can't work. You have to fix the sample immediately. The best method we found was to use dilute formaldehyde to re-hydrate and then use full strength, which fixes it as well as re-hydrating. When you've got the sections, they don't stain like modern tissue. Hyoscine and haemotoxin are used in the lab, the hyoscine stains the cell-cytoplasm and the haemotoxin stains the

nucleus of the cell. We used a lot of other stains as well, but that's the routine one. In mummy tissue that doesn't work very well, so we had to experiment. The proteins in the nucleus have disintegrated, so we experimented with different strengths of these chemicals and we found one of the best was the muscle and connective tissue stain which we used to show up the structure of the mummy tissue, even if the cells had been lost.'

One of the early studies of the mummy team was a new study of the remains of the two brothers whose bodies had been the subject of Margaret Murray's multi-disciplinary study in 1908. Some work on conservation was being carried out on these mummies by the new department, which was set up in 1973 under Frank Goodyear. One of his first projects was to reconstruct the skeleton of Khnum Nakht. He was helped in this project by Roy Garner. They had great difficulties because of the curved spine and deformed foot of the skeleton. Later, when the two brothers were to be displayed with their tomb assemblage, Khnum Nakht had to be placed in a sitting position.

Eddie Tapp became involved in some work on the contents of the canopic jars of Nekht Ankh as the only remaining soft tissue. One interesting result of his study was the discovery of sand pneumoconiosis in the lungs. This has been found in quite a lot of mummies and Dr Tapp wrote it up quite early on in the British Medical Journal. Interestingly a modern link with ancient living conditions emerged, as the condition had been recently described in modern Bedouin and desert people by local health workers. According to Tapp 'of course you don't normally get post-mortems and it just happened that we found it in mummies at the time when it was being described in the modern population.' Nekht Ankh was also found to have suffered from pleurisy

Fig.38 Khnum Nakht sitting up in Manchester Museum

and pericarditis. There were also insect traces associated with his remains, notably evidence of the hump spider beetle which was found inside the bandages, showing that the body must have been exposed for some time before wrapping.

Richard Neave, was a medical artist working in the faculty of Medicine, Dentistry and Nursing. He specialised in painting and drawing specimens for the staff for further study. Many of his subjects came straight from operating theatres or the post mortem room. He used to get warm specimens straight from their source. According to Neave there were no rules on health and safety then. Students could see at firsthand what specimens there were. Neave was recruited to join the team. In his capacity as a medical

artist he was invited to join a group of people mainly from the medical faculty to study the collection of mummified ancient Egyptian people in the Museum. He was obviously impressed by the leader of the project to whom he refers as 'this feisty new star Dr David.' He cannot remember clearly whether the invitation to join in the multi-disciplinary team came from her or someone like Professor Isherwood. Like Rosalie David herself, he feels that Isherwood was a driving force and he might have suggested it. During the on-going study of the two brothers 'we formulated the idea of rebuilding the faces in order to show them off to the general public. The idea was to shape them roughly and then use the heads as a basis from which to make drawings. That was the plan, nothing more.' This approach to the early stages of the work which was to establish a whole new era in the study of human remains, shows the pioneering spirit which was abroad in the Museum.[4]

Neave says, 'great times, we spent an entire weekend casting the skulls - one was easier than the other which had been coated in some sort of glue or something. Nowadays we wouldn't get away with it. We used the technique of wax mailage which we'd used to record malformed babies - we painted them and made them look as if they were alive or fresh. So the techniques were in place to some extent, but we had no facilities. We had to improvise big-time. Nowadays we use the same materials but we're better at it.' He describes the way in which the heads of the two brothers were made. 'We made casts of the two skulls then used modelling clay which was difficult to get hold of in hospital, but we got it. I dredged my brain for all the things I'd done as a student - how do you make plaster of Paris? How much water do you mix with powder to get

---

[4] Neave, Richard, 2007

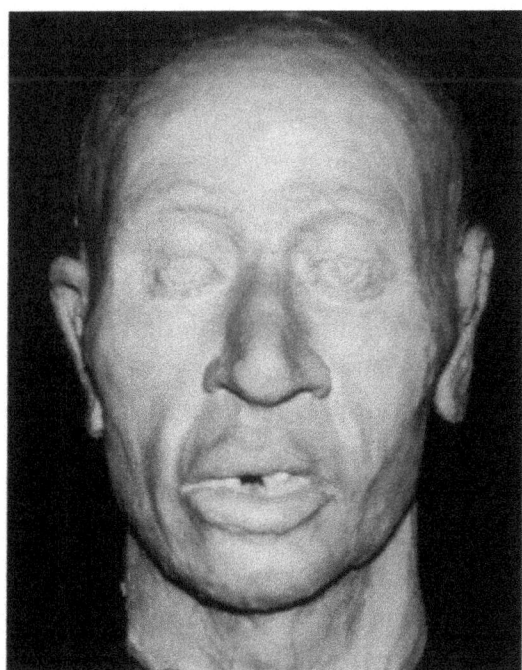

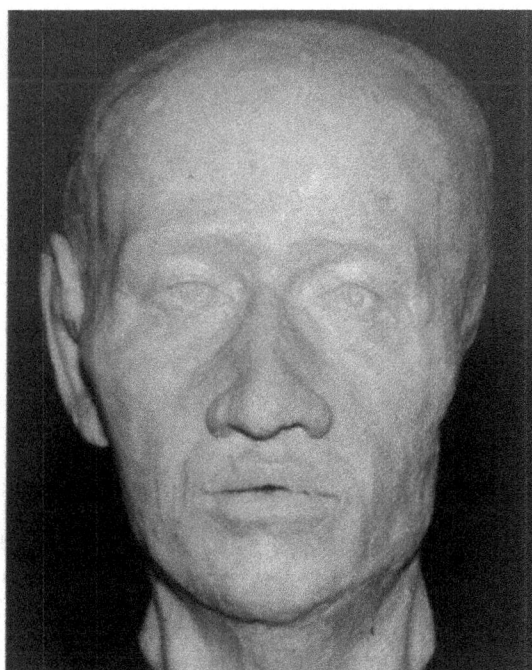

Fig. 39 Reconstructed heads of Khnum Nakht and Nekht Ankh

clay? I built some faces on these two skulls, very crude. I made some drawings but it's hard without the skin. Oddly enough people found it quite interesting.'

The resulting heads showed the different characteristics of the two men, one with an African caste, the other with eunuchoid features. These reconstructions were the first simple examples of this new technique which has been the model for many others, not only of ancient Egyptians but nowadays of modern victims of crime and other mysteries.

13. The unwrapping of Mummy 1770

The public unwrapping of the mummies of Nekht Ankh and Khnum Nakht, the two brothers, by Margaret Murray had been a one-off experiment though it was very important, as it was the first time that a multi-disciplinary team had been assembled for the purpose. After it, however, the remains of the mummies which are now on display in the Museum were reduced to skeletons, a clear illustration of the destructive nature of such methods. Therefore when it was decided to get a multi-disciplinary team to unwrap one of the mummies in 1975, those involved had to balance the value of any information acquired from the procedure against the fact that there might be little left at the end; acquisition of knowledge came at a price. In the late 1960s there had been some studies of mummies in overseas museums such as the autopsies carried out in Detroit on PUM II and in Toronto on ROM I. These had produced some fascinating insights both into health and disease, especially parasitic infestation, and into funerary practices. ROM 1, Nakht, a weaver, for example had been wrapped in his old clothes and had suffered from tapeworms and flat worms, trichinella and taenia.[1] Both these are associated with meat, so provided strong evidence that ordinary Egyptians sometimes had a diet which included meat. These results showed that, although to unwrap a mummy and perform an autopsy on it was necessarily a destructive technique, the amount of important data which could be retrieved was significant. The choice of subject would need to be carefully made however. It was decided to look at a mummy in the Manchester collection which was numbered 1770, about which a great deal was already known. The medical school where they decided to unwrap it was brand new and had huge amounts of laboratory space.

Dr Tapp, the pathologist who took a leading part in the process believes that the authorities allowed them to use this mummy because it was already known to be in a poor state inside its bandages.[2] Earlier X-rays had revealed a problem with the legs; it was clear that one was missing from thigh downwards and the other one from the shin.

The team was composed of clinical and scientific experts. Professor Isherwood, Dr Fawcett and Miss Jarvis dealt with radiological examination while Dr Tapp, did the pathological and histological tests. Dr Curry was responsible for electron-microscopy and Mr Neave was on hand to attempt facial reconstruction. There were experts on embalming (Dr Leach and Mr Garner), breast tissue (Dr Ahmed), paleobiology (Dr Dixon), parasites (Professor Kershaw), textiles (Dr Wild) and Mr Leek, who

had already worked on the heads in the collection, was the team's dental specialist.[3] Such an extensive range of skills had not been assembled before in British Egyptology and the project's aim was to look at the work scientifically and objectively to see what could be found out about disease, how people lived and how they died. Every detail was noted, each bandage was recorded as it was removed and every scrap of tissue was carefully labelled and stored in sealed bags. Insect remains from within the bandages were carefully preserved for future study. Very little soft tissue remained and the abdominal cavity was packed with bandages but there was no sign of internal organs. No amulets were found though these would probably have been present in the original burial. The mummy had been provided with gold finger stalls and, as the rest of the body was revealed, to the great excitement of those present, a pair of beautifully decorated slippers emerged. [4]

The event was fairly public and the presence of the television cameras attracted much attention. According to Richard Neave it took about 5 days to unwrap the mummy. 'There was a whole crowd of the great and the good, the mayor was there and the television people, the media. We were filming it too.' The longer of the two films made by the Audio Visual Service of the University won an award from the British Association for the Advancement of Science.[5] Neave remembered 'the trouble is these things take time. It's not a question of unwrap it, mummy pops out and there you are. It has to be done slowly and scientifically and it took days. So as the days went by, the great and the good gradually dropped off. Stuck in this rather dark laboratory they preferred to be in the sunshine outside and it was left to a few of us, those who had a reasonably dextrous hand and who didn't have a heavy clinical commitment. Eddie Tapp had quite a heavy commitment as a pathologist but even so, he did most of it. I did quite a lot and someone else too'. This other person was Dr Ali Ahmed who was a breast tissue expert, he hoped to find some, but none was found. Nevertheless he was actively involved in the unwrapping, and remembers it as a most interesting experience.[6] Neave comments, 'Rosalie was doing a lot, I was doing some and nobody knew what they were doing. We were making it up as we went along. I remember saying things like one day in ten to fifteen years time we'll have the technology and we won't have to touch these things, we'll be able to see inside.' What an accurate prediction this turned out to be. In the early twenty first century scans and other investigations are regularly carried out on mummies

[1] Hart et al, 1968
[2] David,A.R,1976
[3] Fildes, George, undated.
[4] David, R (ed) 1978
[5] Neave, Richard, 2007
[6] Ahmed ,Ali, Correspondence2006

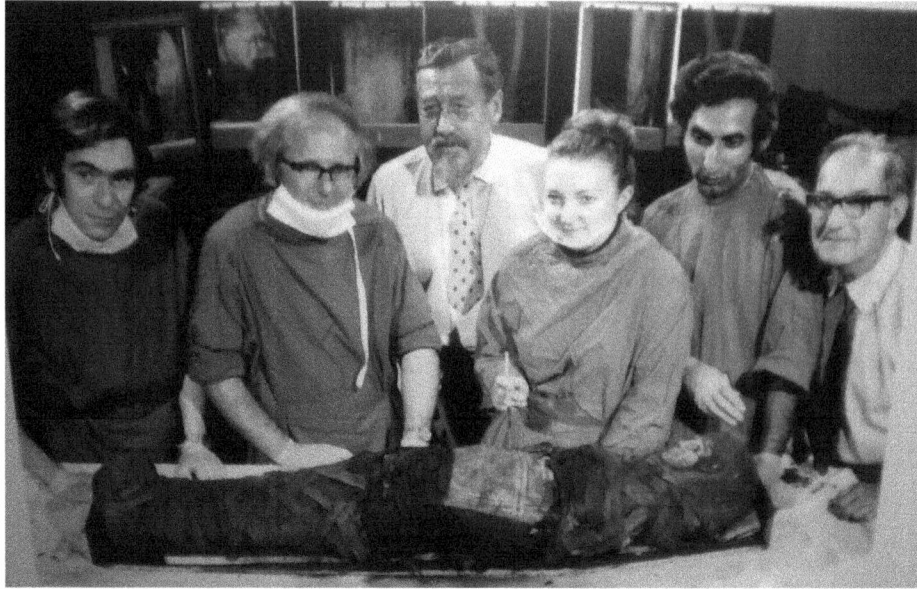

Fig. 40 Rosalie David and her team at the start of the study

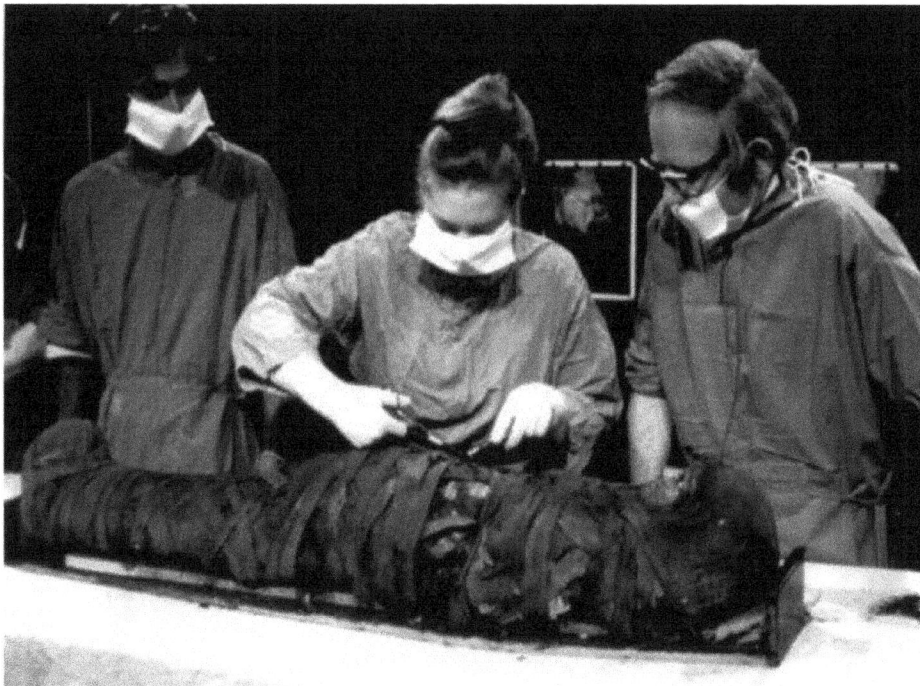

Fig. 41 Rosalie David and Eddie Tapp make the first incision

without damage to their subjects. In 1975 the only way to investigate fully was to unwrap the subject.

The whole project caught the public imagination and within a short time Manchester Museum had become a household name. This was partly due to the influence of television which produced several programmes about the work. One contributory factor to the media interest according to Neave, was that it was a hot summer, England had just lost the test match and the media had little to do,

so they homed in on this in their hordes. It was an ongoing saga for some time, but when it was done, all that could be seen was a pile of broken bones..

As the scientific record shows, there was little visual excitement in the very friable and badly damaged skull which emerged fm the wrappings. The media wanted something to publish which the public would like and find interesting For this reason, Richard Neave was asked to see if he could assemble the skull. He remembers that they

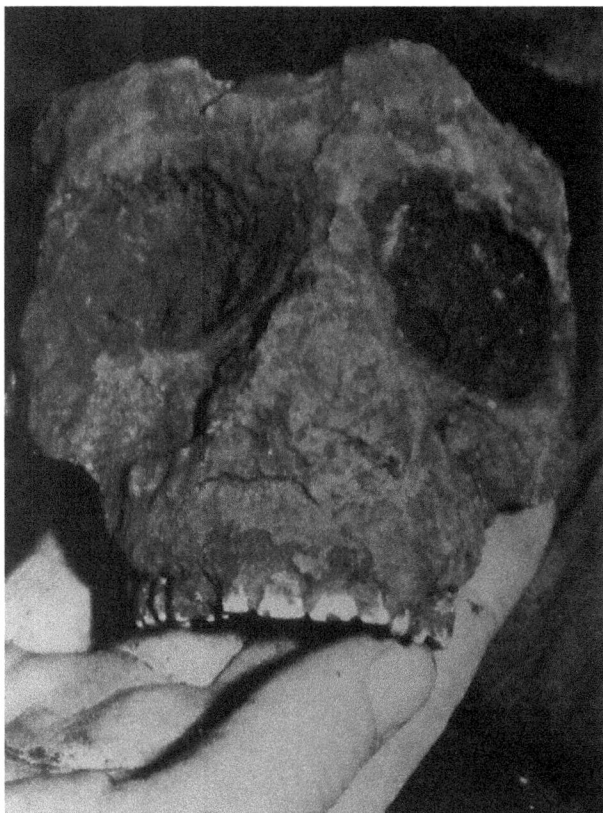

Fig.42 The skull of Mummy 1770

said 'You know those two faces you put on the two brothers
, could you do the same thing with this?' By this time Ian
Isherwood had brought to Neave's attention a paper written
by a professor of anatomy in Liverpool, dating from around
1947 about some work which he had done on Akhenaten.
He had got his medical artist to do some drawings of the
skull and then draw a face over it. He had unearthed some
measurements which had been produced by Kollman &
Buchly, published in the Archives of Anthropology for
1898. Kollman was a scientist and Buchly was a sculptor
which made an interesting collaboration. It is a little
known fact that many scientists working then, actually
had a sculptor to produce the results under their direction.
At that time they were producing tables of soft tissue
measurements. Neave was able to get hold of a copy of the
original data from the British Museum Library and he used
it in the reconstruction of the skull of 1770. He remembers,
'so I had my copy of the skull and I had my measurements
and carried on from there. I put my pegs in and put a bit of
anatomy on it. To me it's the most obvious thing. There's
nothing magical about it. It's much more difficult doing a
portrait sculpture of a living being than it is to reconstruct
a face. For a reconstruction you've got the measurements
and the structure. It's the detail that's missing, really
getting the shape, size and proportions right is hard. The
detail is easy in a real person.'

'What we did is make a model in plaster of this girl. Of
course what we usually did was use wax, for all the dead
babies and so on which we made for the hospital. I went
to the Eye Hospital and asked if I could have a couple of

glass eyes. They told me to help myself but of course eye
hospitals only make glass eyes singly, they don't make them
in pairs!   A bit grisly, but when you think about it, people
don't generally go round with two glass eyes. So I chose
two which were nearly alike, but there is a slight colour
difference. One of my students donated some Rimmel
eyelashes, which girls wore in those days. I went to Boots
where I bought a dark wig and cut a fringe across the front.
I took a bit of surgical bandage and painted it red to tie
round the head, painted the face in the same way we used
to paint the babies. The whole thing was cobbled together
for about 14/6p. Looking back it was rather crude, but it
made the point. If you get the proportions right, it's going
to look right.   People see what they expect to see. The
second point was that something like this has tremendous
impact and fascination for the media. It was phenomenal,
even now the odd head gets a certain amount of coverage
but then it was seen as something quite extraordinary and
remarkable, so pictures of it went everywhere. All sorts of
ramifications from this came about for me personally and
I suppose, for others too. If one is working in a scientific
community rather than an artistic one, the aesthetic merits
of one's work were not even considered, but their accuracy
was. I pursued the accuracy as hard as I could.'

In more recent times reconstructed heads are commonly
displayed, but unlike those made by Richard Neave at that
time, many are now done by computer. It is debateable
whether such efforts can carry the same degree of
realism as those made by a human hand. Neave himself
feels strongly about this and he is quite clear regarding
the limitations even of his technique, as well as more
recent ones. Someone said to him 'the face will be the
same whatever you do. Of course it's not. Everybody
knows that, but there are doubters. We took photographs

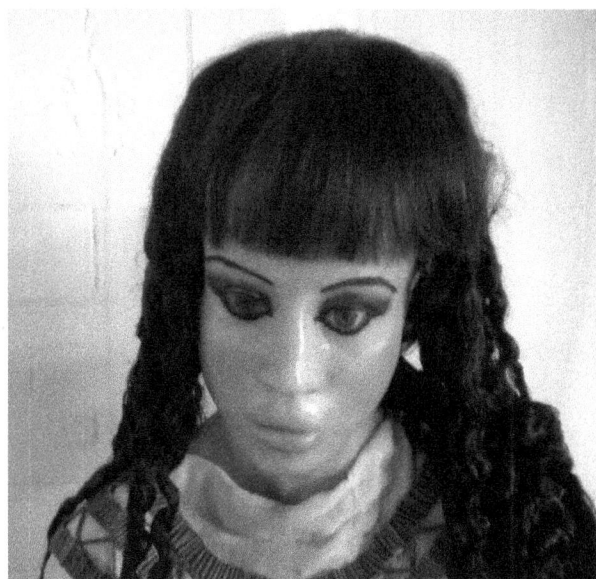

*Fig. 43 Head of 1770 in wax, in store in
Manchester Museum.*

Fig.44 The false leg of 1770

of cadavers before they'd been dissected and then built heads over the skulls. I could never really publish this as they were real people. I was just trying to use what I had. People (the media) tried to imply that the head of 1770 is a totally accurate portrait but of course this can never be so. It is a face which is broadly similar to the original person'. The remains from which he had to work on this head were fragmentary and fragile so it can only be guessed whether she really looked like this in life.

The unwrapping of 1770 produced some important evidence for funerary practices though the customs reflect those of the Roman period rather than the original date of death which was thought to have been satisfactorily proved by radio carbon dating to have been around 1000BC. Very recent work suggests that these dates may not be as definitive as was originally thought. The provenance of this mummy, which arrived in Manchester in 1896 is not certain, though a reference in Petrie's diary and correspondence suggests it probably came from his excavations at Hawara. It will never be known who this person was, and the people who rewrapped the body in the Graeco-Roman period were themselves unsure of the individual's gender since they provided gold nipple covers to allow for lactation in the afterlife and a false penis in case this was a male body.

The amputation of the legs which had been noticed from the X-rays had been compensated for by the provision of false limbs made of mud and sticks.[7] How or why it had taken place became the matter of debate. One theory was that the problem was related to parasitic infestation but Eddie Tapp is not sure. 'Whether that was related to guinea worm is anyone's guess, it could have been.' Other, more dramatic suggestions, such as crocodile attack were raised but the truth is that no-one knows the answer for sure. It became apparent that this mummy had been re-wrapped in antiquity so that the condition of the bodily remains had been affected by post-mortem events. 1770 was just a pile of bones as a result. It was decided from the evidence that the body was actually female and that she had suffered from ill-health all her life. It seems possible

that this unidentified individual was thought by those who rewrapped the remains, to have been a person of some status, perhaps even of royal origin. The most interesting thing to Eddie Tapp was the guinea worm, which Ian Isherwood identified in the original X-rays. [8]

---

[7] David, A.R, 1976

[8] Tapp, Eddie, 2007

14. Looking deeper

After the televising of the unwrapping of mummy 1770, and partly as a result of it, public interest and awareness of the work at the Manchester Museum increased significantly. The work also began to diversify. Those experts who had been involved continued to develop their new techniques and to take advantage of improving technology. Once the first 'Chronicle' television programme had been made, someone suggested that Eddie Tapp and his team should re-hydrate a hand. This was done, and it produced some encouraging results and added to the ever-growing store of knowledge. The work on the mummy known as 1770 had produced some interesting pathology, especially in the area of parasitic infestation. This inspired further study on the other mummies in the collection. Dr Tapp recalls, 'later we started using endoscopes, as I said we needed to be able to get inside the mummies, since the authorities aren't going to let us destroy too many, so I 'borrowed' an old endoscope from the hospital, which we experimented with.'[1] Asru and Khary were the first mummies to be tested in this way. After this, endoscopy was adopted as a central technique, still in use today in mummy studies, because of its non-destructive nature.

Tapp believes that 'it was Rosalie who contacted Ken Wildsmith, who was working for a company which sold endoscopes called Keymed. He was extremely helpful, we couldn't have done the work without him. He provided endoscopes, up to the minute ones.' The mummy of Asru had been unwrapped over a century earlier so the endoscopic study was necessarily limited by its condition. It was possible to examine the thoracic cavity. A study using a small retrieval forceps to take samples of lung tissue revealed a hydatid cyst caused by a parasitic worm in Asru. The same technique, applied later to one of the odd heads in the collection, revealed the same problem. The mummy of Khary, originally famed as the 'oldest passenger on the Ship Canal', was examined in the same way but this study was limited by the fact that the mummy was still partially wrapped. The results allowed samples of lung tissue to be taken and studied. They revealed traces of sand pneumoconiosis, the same condition as that found in Khnum Nakht. Wildsmith and Tapp then turned their attention to the other mummified heads in the Manchester Collection. These studies revealed a great deal of information relating to the techniques used by the embalmers. Several samples revealed resins inside the heads. The use of endoscopes changed the whole approach to mummy investigations. The principle of the endoscope has been known since the early twentieth century but at first, according to Tapp, 'they were horrendous things.' When he was a medical student in the 1950s he remembers

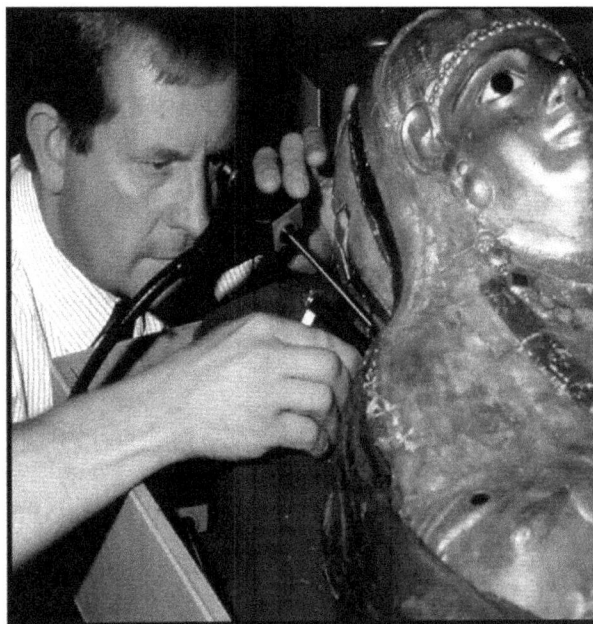

Fig.45 Ken Wildsmith using an endoscope on one of the Manchester mummies.

that they consisted of a thick tube which had to be forced down the throat and because of that they were not used with anything like the frequency they are now. By the 1970s they were a lot more flexible and were getting thinner. As well as this, the fibreglass type which reveals much more information and which could pass right down, had been introduced. Ken Wildsmith supplied different models, including rigid ones like the industrial design which is still used for cystoscopy, investigation of the bladder, but not for other investigations. Ken provided all types including state of the art examples which could video as well as photograph.

The skills of the team were soon in demand from other countries, including Egypt. When the team went to Egypt they had to take their equipment with them in the form of portable endoscopes which were flexible and worked on batteries. This equipment was the subject of much suspicion. As Eddie Tapp recalls, 'the customs wanted them taken to pieces - I think they thought it was a sort of bomb or something'. Such equipment was taken twice in the 1980s. These expeditions were not without difficulty. On the first trip the team went to Cairo to get tissue samples for DNA from bones in store there. The work was not terribly successful as DNA studies were at that time quite new. Another expedition went to Abydos to work with the Australian team led by Naguib Kanawati which had discovered some undisturbed tombs at El-Hagarsa. Rosalie David was attached to the Australian Centre for

[1] Tapp, Eddie, 2008

Egyptology as a Visiting Fellow in 1990 and was invited to bring the skills of her team to bear on the family group of six mummies interred together, in an unusual way apparently at the same time. They dated from about 2200BC and provided an almost unique opportunity for scientific study. The two main objectives of the study by the Manchester team were to try to discover whether the cause of death was disease and to examine the DNA to try to identify family relationships and gender. With the help of a research grant from the British Academy the team set out to take samples for DNA and carry out endoscopic studies. The main survey was carried out in a storehouse at Abydos and tissue and bone samples were brought back to England. The results of these studies were published by The Australian Centre for Egyptology in 1993. It did not prove possible to extract viable DNA from all the mummies, but the four which did yield this, demonstrated surprising results. One, found in a female body coffin and carrying a female name, turned out to be male, while another, in a coffin bearing a male name, proved to be female. This perhaps raises questions about the funerary practices of the embalmers. [2]

Dr Tapp went to Egypt a number of times on similar research projects with Rosalie David and Ken Wildsmith, sometimes not without excitement. He chuckles as he recalls that, 'the third time we went to the Western Desert in 1996, they pushed me down into one of the tombs and I found out afterwards they were full of poisonous snakes. I wouldn't have gone down there if I'd known!' On another occasion they went down into the southern part of Giza and Sakkara. They were guided out into the western desert by an ex-army general who promptly got them lost.

During the 1970s and 1980s extensive work was carried out not only on the mummies from the Manchester collection but also on examples from other museums, work which continues to the present day. The team deployed every technique available at the time, to add to the data already known. Not only were endoscopic examinations a central part of the process but also histology, analysis of blood groups, and detailed dental study. Much of the early work is reported in 'Evidence Embalmed', published in 1984.[3] The examination of the Leeds mummy, that of Natsef Amun, allowed the application of more innovative techniques. This mummy, of a priest, had been the subject of one of the very earliest scientific studies in the 1820s. Now it was subjected to a battery of modern methods. Computed tomography (CT) scans revealed that he had degenerative arthritis of the hip as well as severe wear on the teeth, a common feature in the population of ancient Egypt.

One of the techniques used, involving electron microscopy revealed a wealth of information, not only about the life and death of the Egyptians but also the funerary practices in use. The results of studies on mummified material gave some indication of how far body parts had putrefied before

embalming. The degree of preservation of some liver tissue from one of the two brothers for example, showed that it had been removed and dried soon after death. Brain tissue from an isolated head on the other hand revealed that the brain had putrefied before being removed. Analytical electron microscopy allowed the team to investigate the presence of non-organic materials in the tissues. In the case of Nekht Ankh the presence of crystalline structures containing silicon, iron and titanium in the lungs provided evidence of sand pneumoconiosis.

One of the significant outcomes of the working together of the mummy team both in those early days and now, is how many experts, originally not connected with Egyptology at all, have become deeply involved. Dr Tapp and his wife both did the Egyptology certificate course in the University and, although he has little time nowadays to pursue it, he retains the enthusiasm which was engendered by their studies. He has a high opinion of the course and has been impressed by the extent of its influence. Once, when called to the scene of a murder at midnight in his capacity as a Home Office Pathologist, he found himself working with two young female local pathologists. 'I don't think I know you' he said. 'But we know you,' was the reply, 'you lectured to us when we were doing the Egyptology Certificate!'

[2] Kanawati, Naguib et al. 1993 pp85-86
[3] David, Rosalie and Tapp,Eddie,(eds.) 1984

15. Heads, teeth and hands

The data revealed by scans allowed the development of a new and improved method of reconstructing the head of the mummy using the three-dimensional views. These were translated into solid form by using a computer controlled milling machine to carve a replica of the skull. Richard Neave's final head of Natsef Amun (Nesy Amun) revealed a strong face, probably reflecting a Nubian heritage. He felt that it was a great improvement on his earlier attempts at reconstruction. He comments that 'the Two Brothers were pretty crude'.

The head of Natsef Amun was the last of Neave's Egyptian heads for Manchester, though after this, he did a couple more for the British Museum, these were examples from the Fayoum with portraits on them. The aim of this work was to see whether the reconstructions looked like the portraits. He did the portrait head of another local celebrity, Lindow Man, and now specialises in pathology cases for the police, as a result of which in many cases, the victim has been successfully identified. As he said, 'occasionally one struck lucky, sometimes the result is more accurate than one might expect.' [1]

Neave's successor, Caroline Wilkinson still works with the ongoing mummy studies although she is now based in Dundee in the Centre for Anatomy and Human Identification. The techniques of facial reconstruction have come a very long way from the early days, not least because of the development of computers. Three-dimensional models may now be produced from radiographs or photographs, or a combination of the two, as well as from actual skull remains.

One of the most enduring parts of a body, whether embalmed or naturally decayed, is the dentition. Teeth can be of great value in assessing not only the dental health of an individual, but also the general health and, in some cases, can even provide a clue to the cause of death. Modern methods can also allow the extraction of DNA from dental material. Studies of ancient Egyptian teeth in Manchester have been a major part of the research. The late Frank Filce Leek made an outstanding contribution from the 1960s onwards. He had already had a notable career in dentistry and had built up an international reputation before becoming involved in Egyptology. He was also a man of wide interests including ornithology and the archaeology of Roman Britain. When he retired he took up Egyptology with enthusiasm and from 1963 onwards he made many visits to Egypt with his wife and later, with Eddie Tapp and his wife, with whom they became friendly. They used to visit the dig sites of eminent Egyptologists

Fig.46 Reconstructed head of Natsef Amun.

like Emery and take welcome English provisions such as Red Label Tea. According to Leek's daughter, Lesley, he was involved in filming 'Chronicle' programmes with Magnus Magnusson in Egypt. One of these programmes included a sequence filmed at his home with Mrs Leek cooking ancient Egyptian food. Being a typical enthusiast, he also carried out experiments in brain removal using sheep's heads.

In 1968 he had helped Harrison in Liverpool with his examination of the mummy of Tutankhamun before joining the research in the Manchester Museum, and was author of a steady stream of academic papers, many published in the Journal of Egyptian Archaeology.[2] In 1975 he joined the Manchester Mummy Team and made a significant contribution to its findings. He examined all the Manchester mummies' X-rays and was able to draw important conclusions from what was revealed. One interesting point which emerged from his study was the general lack of caries, or tooth decay, before the Ptolemaic period. In the case of 1770, for example, he observed that the lack of any major wear on the teeth and the mal-positioning of some of them, suggested that the young

---

[1] Neave, Richard 2007

[2] Dixon, D.M., in JEA 1986

woman had not eaten normal Egyptian food. She may have had to live on a liquid or semi-liquid diet. In other mummies there was evidence of severe dental problems. Khary, for example, had abscesses under five of his teeth and the surface of others was worn right down to the pulp. Experiments conducted in the 1960s by John Prag had been designed to prove the theory that grit was added to the grain in order to aid the grinding process. Although more recent studies seem to prove otherwise, there is no doubt that grit, whether deliberately added or accidentally added from the flint sickles used in harvesting, or wind-blown particles, played a part in the generally poor state of dental health.

Besides the Manchester mummies, Frank Leek was able to gain access to large collections of skulls. Elliot Smith's skulls from Nubia and a collection of skulls kept in Giza, which showed a representative population of the nobility of the Old Kingdom, provided an opportunity to make some assessment of the life and health of a whole community. Of 118 skulls studied, 63 were adult males, 38 were adult females and 17 were juveniles or infants. Despite the fact that the jawbones had been separated, making matching a time consuming and ultimately pointless exercise, many interesting conclusions could be reached. Little dental decay was present but there was a high incidence of abscesses, probably due to severe wear of the teeth. It appeared from the evidence that the Egyptians did not realise the connection between pain and swelling of the facial tissues and the presence of a hidden abscess.

The population apparently kept up some standard of dental health, perhaps using the frayed end of a stick. In

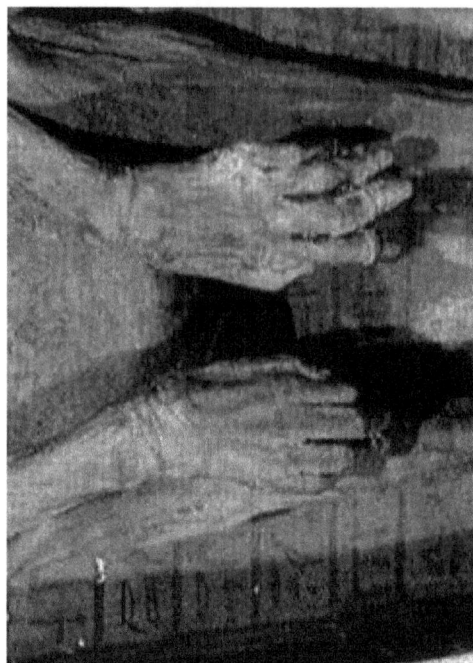

Fig.47 Asru's hands

the Rylands Papyrus, which is kept in the John Rylands Library, there is even a recipe for tooth powder, since this is in Greek however, it may be that the idea of oral hygiene came rather late to Egypt. Generally speaking, those individuals who had died before about twenty-five years of age did not have serious dental problems, but these became increasingly common with the ageing process. Dr Leek made many studies of dry skulls, both in Egypt and

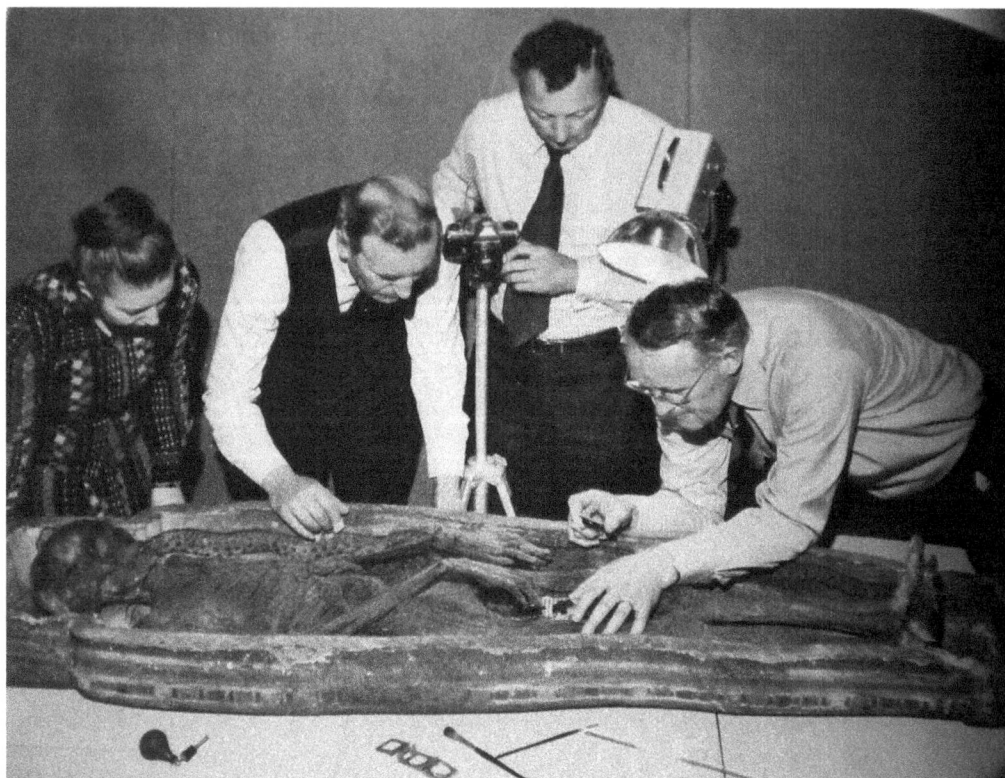

Fig.48 Taking Asru's fingerprints

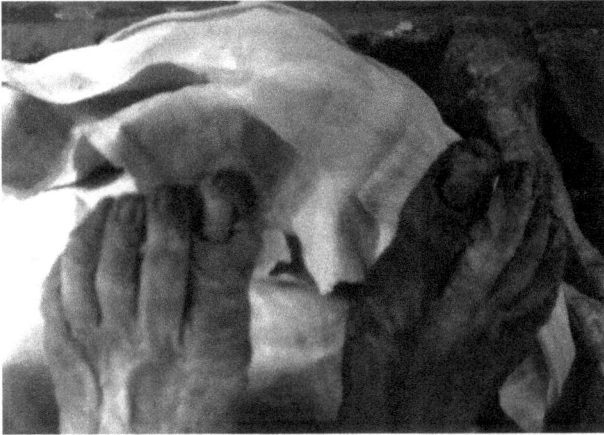

Fig. 49 Asru's feet

in museums in many locations, and found that the general conclusions which could be drawn, applied to most classes and to most periods of history.

The pioneering work of the Manchester Team has sometimes had far-reaching effects outside Egyptology. The methods devised by them for taking fingerprints from mummies has been used in police work to identify decayed human remains and is known as the Manchester Method. Fingerprints are not only important for identifying individuals, but may give important clues as to lifestyle. It is well known that fingerprints are unique to each person, but it is less obvious that the swirls and loops that appear clearly to be on the surface or epidermis, are actually retrievable from the layer underneath. This is particularly important when the surface layer is damaged, as may happen in the case of a mummified body.

In order to study the prints of Asru, the Chantress of Amun, new methods of taking prints had to be developed, since the rigid position of the hands and the fragility of the remains meant that conventional methods were not appropriate. Experimental techniques were devised and tried out on other fingers that were in the collection. The hands of Asru were carefully photographed through a mirror placed face up under the fingers. After this, a compound, which was at the time used in dental work, was delicately placed on each finger and later on the feet. From this quick-drying, but easily removable material, a cast of the print emerged, which was then coated with several layers of black acrylic paint. The resulting cast could then be used to take prints with ink, as if fingers were directly inked and printed in the conventional way. Similar methods were used to take casts of the toes and the soles of the feet. The study of these casts allowed conclusions to be drawn about Asru's professional life since there had been some question as to whether she had been a singer or a dancer. The lack of wear or callousing of the feet made it fairly clear that she had not been a dancer, only a chantress.

By chance, as this work was proceeding, the police were alerted to the discovery of a man's partially decomposed body in Rochdale. In order to identify it, the Mummy Team's fingerprint technique was applied, leading to the identification of the individual. Following this success, the Greater Manchester Police adopted these new techniques as standard practice, for use with unidentified human remains and they have also been adopted by other forces.[3]

Manchester was now at the forefront of Egyptological research and, reflecting this, held a symposium in 1979 and again in 1984. The papers given at these symposia came from a wide range of academic institutions. The 1979 symposium marked the end of the first phase of the Mummy Project, which had now achieved international renown. It had been the subject of a film made by the Central Office of Information, for distribution overseas, in which the innovative techniques established in Manchester were shown to have contributed to forensic work and plastic surgery.[4]

The last word here rests with the late Frank Leek who concluded his contribution in the 1979 report, by acknowledging in print that the main influence came from Dr David. 'The help and consideration given by Dr A. Rosalie David has been outstanding and I also wish to pay tribute to her leadership of 'The Team'. It has been a delightful and interesting experience to work with them all.'[5]

---

[3] David, R. (ed) 1979
[4] David, R and Tapp, E,(eds),1984
[5] Leek, F. Filce in David,(ed) 1979, p. 77

16. Invaders and unwelcome guests

Much can be learned from organic remains found in and around mummies which were not human in origin. These either provide clues to the health and life-style of the person or they give clues to the processes of funerary practice and natural decay. Endoscopy and microscopy have revealed much important data on both these areas. Some samples provided evidence of the presence of parasites in the bodies while other studies were made of the insect remains associated with the mummified material.

With 1770, whose remains had been rewrapped many centuries after her death, for example, there were traces of several flies and beetles including the common house fly, the carabid beetle and the cheese skipper which breeds in meat and cheese. One of the problems of this type of study is to decide whether the insects date from the time of death or perhaps later. Woodworm was found in coffin wood which may have arrived at a much later time while the cheese skipper (*piophila*) could well have infested the dead body itself at an early stage since it is a pest of stored meat. 1770 was also infested with guinea worm.[1] This is ingested in its immature form with drinking water. The male dies after mating in the abdominal area while the pregnant female migrates, often settling in the legs where its presence causes ulcers. The eggs are then laid in the ulcers allowing the young to escape into water where the whole process is repeated. Many of the diseases which have been traced during the course of the Mummy Project of have been the result of parasitic infestation. The most frequent of these is hydatid disease from a dog tapeworm whose life cycle starts in sheep. If one is ingested, it does not become a tapeworm. The eggs go to a part of the body and form large cysts in the lungs and, as in the case of Asru, the brain. This poor lady was also found to have been infested with the *strongyloides* worm which, in the same way as schistosomiasis, has a life-cycle beginning in water. Its immature form penetrates the skin and the organism spreads through the body until it reaches its mature form, in the case of Asru, in her intestines. These water-borne parasites are still endemic and, being particularly prevalent in standing water, present a threat to the modern population of agricultural workers. Almost all mummies studied show the presence of at least one parasite and frequently several different types. The Leeds Mummy, Nesy Amun, when subjected to a complete autopsy by the Manchester Mummy Team, showed an infestation by *filaria*, a parasite which blocks the lymphatic vessels. This can sometimes lead to elephantiasis and may account for the curious appearance of the Queen of Punt as painted on the wall of Hatshepsut's funerary temple at Deir el Bahri.[2]

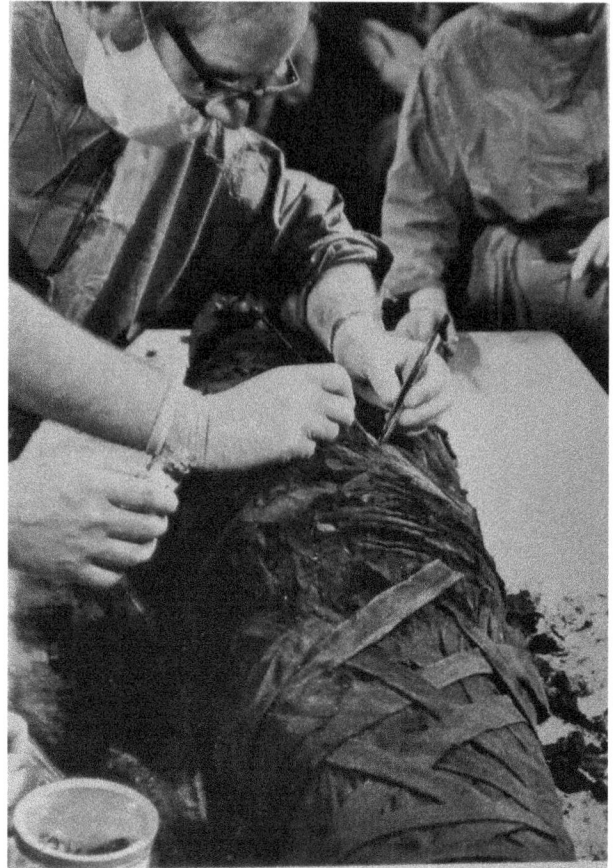

Fig. 50 Removing insect remains from Mummy 1770

External parasites can also be found. In a very recent study of the mummy of Takabuti in the KNH Centre, she was found to be infested with insects, although it could not be determined if they were modern or ancient. A possible louse or nit egg, however, was found attached to one hair strand. It was not feasible at that stage to say definitely that she was infested with nits, as the sample was very small. A specimen mounted on a slide for microscopy can become distorted. However, this did appear to be a louse egg, on the basis of the characteristic oval shape cemented to the hair shaft. Later tests showed that the first impression was incorrect. What looked like an egg was not what it seemed. This underlines the difficulties faced by researchers when the quality or quantity of evidence is inadequate for the purpose. Takabuti, like many of her ancient Egyptian contemporaries may well have suffered with head lice. There are traditional remedies to treat lice, similar to the contemporary methods used today. The hair is covered with an oil to suffocate the lice, which along with the eggs are removed by a fine toothed comb.[3]

---

[1] David, R (ed) 1978
[2] David, Rosalie And Tapp, Eddie, (eds.)1984

---

[3] McCreesh, Natalie, 2009

One of the common parasitic invaders which affected the ancient Egyptians and continues to be a major problem today is schistosomiasis. The eggs of the schistozome parasite are carried by a variety of water-borne snail. The hatched larvae are released into the water where they find human hosts. They enter the skin through the hair follicles and turn immediately into worms. These travel to the liver where they breed to produce a new generation of eggs which are laid in the intestine or the bladder. The consequences of a severe infestation can be serious, leading to blood in the urine, calcification of the bladder, fibrosis of the intestine or cirrhosis of the liver. The eggs may then be replaced in the water through excretion and the cycle begins again. Written evidence, in, for example, the Ebers Medical Papyrus, suggests that this was a common problem in ancient times. In line with its tradition of innovative methods, the Manchester team began to research this.

In 1996, Rosalie David, seeing a logical progression from the study of ancient remains, joined forces with the Egyptian Ministry of Health, and Medical Service Corporation International, a company based in Arlington, Virginia, which specialises in medical services in the developing world. The aim of the project, using the resources of the Manchester Mummy Team, was to study for the first time, the evolution of a single disease over five thousand years. In order to gather evidence, there was a need to study as much mummy tissue as possible. This required a system of preserving such data, which resulted in the setting up of the International Mummy Tissue Bank, where around 1400 human hair and tissue samples currently provide a research resource for scholars world-wide. Patricia Lambert, one of the post-doctoral students, who set out to locate every known mummy outside Egypt, carried out the initial work on this. It was a new departure for her, since she had done her PhD research into mummification rituals.[4] Her work at Manchester Museum was funded by the Leverhulme Foundation, which has made major contributions to mummy studies in Manchester over recent years.

Patricia Lambert began searches to locate any human remains held by museums and private collections with a view to recording this information, but also to persuade establishments to participate in the project by providing tissue samples for the Tissue Bank. This was originally held in the Museum in an old document safe in the mummy store. It was, and is, essential to provide a controlled, sealed environment in order to protect the organic material and to ensure that the air exchange is also regulated. Samples in the collection are tiny, since they need to be taken in a non-destructive way. Ideally these samples consist of one or two grams of dry tissue from several body sites of an authenticated Egyptian mummy, preferably including a hair sample. If bladder or intestine samples are also provided, this can be of great benefit to the Schistosomiasis Project. Some samples are on slides but most of them are in

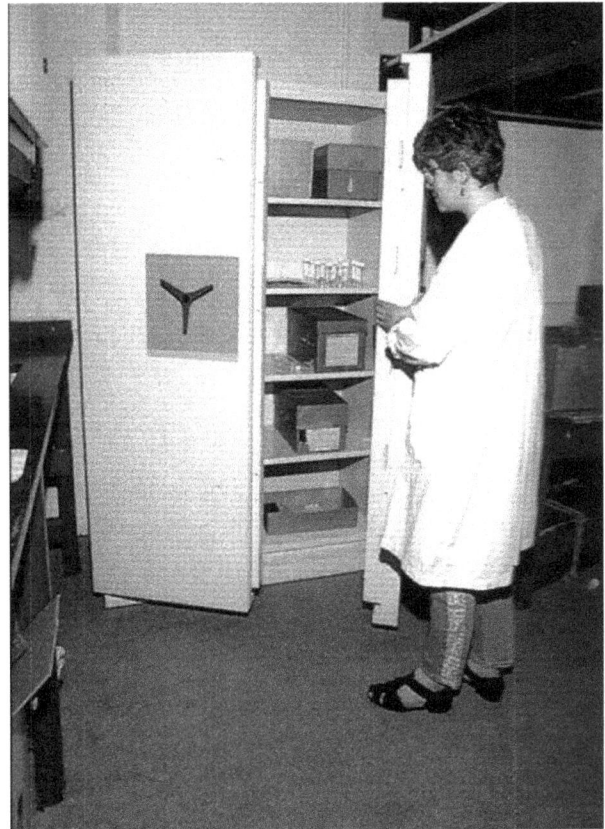

Fig.51 Patricia Lambert with the first Mummy Tissue Bank

plastic bags. Mummy tissue is a finite source so methods, like those used by the investigating teams throughout the project, must be as non-invasive as possible. Researchers may have access to the material, provided they undertake not to compromise it in any way.

A suitably controlled environment is being provided now that the KNH Centre has moved to its permanent home in the Faculty of Life Sciences. It is hoped that in the longer term, the bank will be joined by a complementary collection to include samples of other organic materials including bone, resins and plant materials. This will provide an important further resource for research into pharmacy, medicine and embalming methods. A computerised catalogue will keep detailed data on each sample.[5]

The Schistosomiasis Project involved the study of data collected from around 100,000 people living in villages in modern Egypt. Manchester's role was to investigate samples of mummified tissue to try to identify epidemiological evidence for ancient populations. The hope was that comparison of ancient and modern patterns of parasitic disease might provide clues as to how to treat the disease, still rife in Egypt. In order to identify schistosomiasis traces in the tiny samples available, it was essential to develop a method, or protocol to achieve this.

Another PhD student in her doctoral and later post-doctoral work developed such a method. Patricia Rutherford was

---

[4] Lambert Zazulak, Patricia, interview 2005

[5] David, Rosalie (ed), 2008

one of the first graduates of the newly established MSc course in Biomedical and Forensic Studies in Egyptology, which was another of Rosalie David's innovations. Rutherford's specialism is immunocytochemistry, which aims to study chemical changes in disease infected cells. Having only tiny samples to work with, she had to find a way of discovering traces of disease. Instead of looking for antibodies in the samples, she decided to look for the antigen, or invading entity, by developing an anti-serum to search it out. She describes this process in layman's terms as being 'like bloodhounds that unerringly track down a suspect.'[6] Having tracked the offender, the next step is to stain the tissue and to examine it under the microscope. Dr Rutherford's first ancient test case was the mummy numbered 1766 in the Manchester Collection. This is a female mummy from the Fayoum dating from around 1800BC, which was found to have been severely infected over a long period of time. Other studies on groups of mummies from the Dahkleh Oasis and the Sudanese Desert suggest that there is not much difference in levels of infection between the rich and the poor. In a modern population it is the poor who suffer most.

Dr Rutherford found that the isolation of suitable tissue presented problems, since mummy tissue is either leathery or very brittle. It requires rehydration before it can be studied using the protocol that was being developed. Months of dedicated experiment eventually produced the answer - fabric softener! The commercial version of this however, contained perfume and other additives, which could have affected her results, so she had to find a version that had none. Another problem in studying ancient tissue is the presence of sand in the samples. Using a resource that was available to her, namely the chemical plant where her husband worked, she was eventually able to find a solution to this problem, allowing her to produce high-grade slides for study. This long process was crowned with success and provided a foolproof method for identifying schistosomiasis in ancient tissue, a real breakthrough in mummy studies.

Subsequent work has revealed that 30% of the mummy samples examined contained traces of the schistosome parasite. Studies of the organs of the Dahkleh group are continuing and revealing more information. An interesting suggestion is that the infestations seem more widespread in the younger people, since they perhaps spent more time in the water.

The work had developed further into the area of DNA research. The survival of ancient DNA is dependent upon the conditions in which a sample has survived. For example, rapid desiccation, as in the process of mummification, can result in good preservation of DNA samples.[7] This is particularly true of skin samples, since the skin would be the first part of the body to dry out. Frequently however, the samples are damaged or very small and contamination by other DNA is an ever-present

hazard. Many herbs and spices were used in the process of embalming so that plant DNA might confuse the results of tests. There is also an ethical consideration; extraction of DNA samples may result in the total destruction of the tissue, thus making replication of the tests impossible and reducing the available amount of material for future researchers. The aim is to be able to extract enough DNA from ancient samples, so that modern forms of the parasite may be compared with it, gene by gene. This will provide clues to the evolution of such organisms and could lead to important breakthroughs, possibly helping in the fight to find a cure.

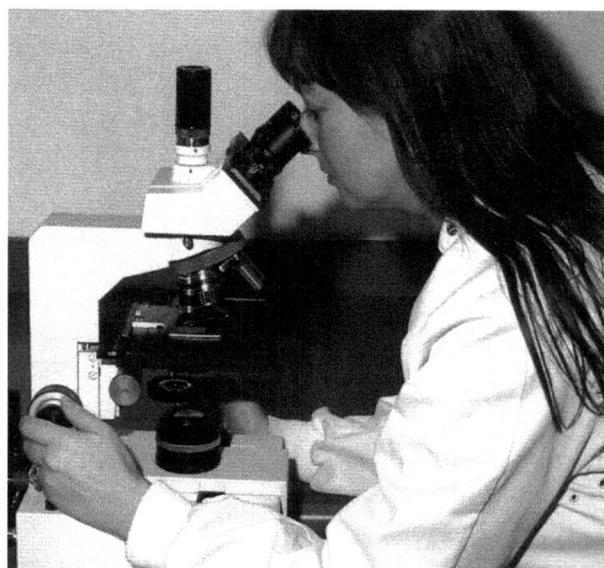

Fig. 52 Patricia Rutherford at work

---

[6] Archbold, Rick and David, Rosalie, 2000
[7] Rutherford, Patricia in David, Rosalie (ed), 2008

17. The origins of the KNH Centre

One of Rosalie David's regular commitments is to accompany a tour of Egypt as lecturer in residence. This suits her informal style well, and travellers over the years have benefitted from her clear and interesting talks on many aspects of ancient Egyptian history. One of these beneficiaries was a Yorkshire woman who went on the tour in the early nineties. She became completely hooked and resolved to pursue her interest. She was to become the generous benefactor of the KNH Centre for Biomedical Egyptology. Like her predecessor, Jesse Haworth, she prefers to keep out of the limelight, and does not wish too much to be written about her.

She says 'well I saw Rosalie's ambition and qualities, I thought, everyone is here to make the world a better place. Here's my opportunity to make progress, to do something different.' She explains, 'You see my father always said to me it's not money that's evil, it's what you do with it. But when you sell a company, which I wasn't expecting, you have money at your disposal. Rosalie has given me an opportunity to do something constructive with it.'[1] The aim was purely to use the fund for the advancement of science. The result was the establishment of the KNH Centre for Biomedical Egyptology in the Faculty of Life Sciences in the University of Manchester. It was opened officially by

the Earl of Wessex in 2006. This is now the centre of a vast programme of research headed by its Professor, Rosalie David.

When questioned about how the idea was realised K. emphasises the chance nature of her meeting with Rosalie David who acknowledges that chance played a part, but believes that their encounter was fruitful because of the timing. The fact that the University was able to accept the concept at that point, meant that an idea which might not have been feasible at another juncture could be implemented. In the same way, Amelia Edwards' introduction of Jesse Haworth to Flinders Petrie had happened at the most opportune moment. According to Peggy Drower, Petrie's biographer, Petrie seems to have had an idea for a northern project in Egyptology, perhaps with its own Professor. An article in the John Rylands bulletin said that Jesse Haworth had a hope when he gave the collections to the Museum that the gift would be mirrored by the establishment of a teaching department. However after Margaret Murray left, Egyptology, apart from the collections, became sidelined and the Chair was never created. Now, with the help of the KNH Trust, the teaching department has been established and the Chair came into being.

Its holder, Rosalie David is warm in her commendation. She believes that K. has given a great deal to so many people's lives, particularly young people. She has opened

---

[1] KNH 2006

Fig.53 Caroline Wilkinson meets the Earl of Wessex while Rosalie David looks on.

up their futures and laid a foundation for ongoing work. 'K. had already been very supportive in different ways but then the situation developed and she said she could do something really very major. She said what do you think would really be the best thing to do, and I said, out of the blue, well it would be a centre with a Chair. Manchester has everything except that, and when Jesse Haworth gave the collection he believed the square would be rounded if that could be done and that was always the dream.'[2]

So the dream has been fulfilled and following the long and highly respected tradition of Egyptological work at the University of Manchester, the KNH Centre is the focus of national and international attention. It is the only University department in Britain where Egyptology can be studied through the biological sciences rather than as an historical study in the classical tradition or through its language and material culture. It provides educational and research opportunities to post-graduate students studying for MSc and PhD degrees. Most recently the University Certificate in Egyptology, which has been an inspiration to many members of the public in the Centre for Continuing Education in the Faculty of Arts, has been transferred to the KNH Centre. Following the tradition of employing the most up-to date methods available, it is currently a distance learning course, entirely on line.

[2] David, Rosalie, 2006

18. The work of the KNH Centre

When the KNH Centre was first set up, the work already in progress at the Museum on organic remains was transferred, together with the researchers involved. Patricia Lambert and Patricia Rutherford continued to develop the Mummy Tissue Bank and the Schistosomiasis Project respectively. Researchers in the University of Cairo now study the modern disease and those in Manchester study the ancient examples. It is anticipated that research will move on to Malaria and other diseases caused by parasites.

Nowadays the centre is involved in a comprehensive range of international work. Some of this is in partnership with the National Research Centre in Cairo, which is the leading government science centre in Egypt. The Faculty of Life Sciences has set up a formal agreement with it which has developed into a regular exchange of students and staff and there is now an annual workshop in Cairo, training new generations of local students and staff in Bio-medical Egyptology. There will be a body of people to carry the subject forward when those who pioneered it have gone.

In Turin, the University Department of Anthropology, working with the Museum, forms a third partner in this arrangement with the National Research Centre in Cairo. Turin has an outstanding collection of Egyptian material and a Museum dedicated to its display. The partners collaborate on researching the collection of mummies in the Museum adopting a similar approach to the work being done in Manchester. The hope is that future projects may be possible which will involve all three countries.

Research projects which have been, or are in process of, being developed are wide-ranging. They include studies on several types of DNA, diseases such as sickle-cell anaemia, parvo-viral malaria as well as schistosomiasis, thoracic bacteria and therapeutic treatments. Forensic studies on hair, possible dyes, resins and salts such as natron have all been carried out as well as work on animal mummies and fungal growth in remains. Other studies involve the evaluation of radio carbon dates. Every new student brings a fresh perspective and some of their creative approaches have established new protocols for research.

The main driving force in the development of Egyptology in Manchester since 1972, Rosalie David, has provided the inspiration and leadership for all the major projects which have been and still are being carried out in Manchester.

Rosalie was born in Cardiff in 1946, the daughter of a sea captain. Her interest in Egyptology began at a very young age. She attended Howell's School in Llandaff. After leaving school, she studied Ancient History and Egyptology at University College London and then went on to Liverpool University to study for a PhD. She chose

Fig. 54 Rosalie David OBE, Professor of Egyptology.

Liverpool because she was interested in comparative religion in which the department specialized. Her research on the religious rituals of the ancient Egyptians as recorded on the walls of the Temple of Seti I at Abydos meant that she had to spend long periods of time in Egypt. While she was there she met many interesting people including the legendary Umm Seti, an Englishwoman who served the temple of Seti I believing herself to be a reincarnation of an ancient hand-maiden. A more important meeting while she was there, was her introduction to her future husband, Antony. They married in 1970 and have worked together on many projects over the years. He is a conservator and has worked for the North West Museum and Art Galleries Service based in Blackburn and subsequently with Lancashire County Museums Service. Now retired from full-time work, he takes an active part in the KNH Centre, teaching the students techniques of conserving mummies.[1]

Professor David's innovative and broadly-based approach to mummy studies has made Manchester pre-eminent in the field, laying a foundation which is being built upon by succeeding generations. She started the Virtual Kahun Project, linked up with the Petrie Museum. This was a computerized interactive programme which used the remarkable collection of material in the Manchester Museum from Petrie's excavations at Kahun. It continues, but now under the aegis of the Petrie Museum in London.

When she first came to work at the Manchester Museum, she also held an honorary lectureship in the Comparative Religion Department, as it was then called. She taught on the three year undergraduate course and also taught some post graduates studying for MPhil and PhD degrees. Her certificate course, offered to the public in the Extra-Mural Department, spread the fascination for Egyptology far and wide.

In 1995 Dr David and her Mummy Team decided they needed to train a new generation and they believed that the obvious course of action was to set up a new MSc degree. This idea had been advanced before, but the pure scientists were unhappy about the Arts element, so had sent the proposal back for further thought. It is a measure of Rosalie David's vision that in fact the MSc programme which is now running successfully in the KNH Centre is popular with students from both science and arts backgrounds.

There came a point in her career where she felt she had achieved all she could in Manchester so she began to look elsewhere. Fortunately for Manchester, this galvanized some of those who had followed the work of the Mummy Project closely and some academic scientists, into setting up the MSc course she wanted, in collaboration with the Department of Biological Sciences. She had a room there and an honorary Readership for a three year period. A few years later her achievements were recognized in the form of the award of a Professorial Chair. She was the first female Professor of Egyptology in Britain.

Her influence has been very widely felt, not only in research and teaching. Over the years she has been responsible for forging links world-wide through co-operative projects and International Symposia on Science in Egyptology. These links continue to grow and develop now that her work has moved into the KNH centre which is physically located in the Stopford Building, the Medical School of the University.

It is a mark of her achievements that many of the people interviewed for this book made a special point of emphasizing the positive influence she has had on their lives. Examples include someone who said, 'X did Rosalie's course - it changed his life and I wouldn't be doing what I do without Rosalie's course'. Another said

'all the way along she supports you, any side learning she encourages.' She is said to be 'way ahead in her thinking' and 'wonderfully encouraging with young people. She gives chances in the department'. There is no doubt that she has a knack of maximizing people's talents and boosting their confidence.

At the time of writing there are three others employed in the KNH Centre as staff members. Angela Thomas who used to be at Bolton Museum is now the Honorary Teaching Fellow. She believes her interest in Egyptology goes back to her father who was in the army in Egypt and Libya after the war. The family visited Cairo and the pyramids when she was between 9 and 12 years old. After her father's premature death in an accident they came back to England. Her headmistress thought she should do something socially useful which Egyptology was not considered to be, so after her schooling, she began to study Law at Dundee, then part of St. Andrews. Law did not suit her, so after two years she asked to transfer to Liverpool where her father came from. She took up combined studies with Egyptology and French as main subjects and Prehistoric Archaeology, under Professor Fairman and Terence Powell. She first met Rosalie David, who had just come from London as a postgraduate. After a temporary job at Liverpool Museum under Dorothy Downs, she got a curator's job at Buckinghamshire County Museum in Aylesbury, where there was a small Egyptian collection. After two years she decided to do a higher degree, rather than the Museum Diploma. A job came up in Bolton and her Professor, Harry Smith, said 'there are few jobs and nothing in London and you come from the North, why don't you try it?' Having been appointed, her intention was to stay for a few years and then move on but circumstances led to her staying until she retired in 2005, and she joined the KNH Centre soon afterwards.[2]

Joyce Tyldesley divides her time between the KNH Centre, as Lecturer in Egyptology, and the Manchester Museum where she is concerned with outreach to the public, organising seminars. Joyce was not originally an Egyptologist, although her interests always leant in that direction. She believes that living in the North West, which allowed access to the outstanding Egyptian collections in the Bolton and Manchester Museums, triggered her interest in ancient Egypt. She remembers visiting the Museum when she was about six years old. She recalls rather wryly a school trip to the Tutankhamun Exhibition in the early seventies. The group actually had tickets but they had no time to go round the exhibition. Rosalie David visited her school on the day when she went back to pick up her A-level certificate and that was the first time she heard her speak. She never dreamed that one day they would be working together. She attended Bolton School, taking Science 'A' levels with a view to doing medicine. Instead, she decided to do Archaeology, but never really expected it to be a proper job. She felt it would be a very good background for many other things, so the plan was

---

[1] David, Rosalie 2005

[2] Thomas, Angela, 2007

Fig. 55 Joyce Tyldesley (centre) and Jacqueline Campbell with Roger Forshaw.

to go on to something else like accountancy or law. At Liverpool University, she wanted to do the Prehistory and Egyptology modules together but this was not an option at the time, much to her annoyance, as she really wanted to do the Prehistory of Egypt. After graduating in Prehistory, she went on to Oxford to do a doctorate specialising in British prehistoric flints. She had done some fieldwork in Egypt with the British Museum and some with Stephen Snape her husband, in the Delta. In addition, she had her own EES studentship to do some work at Tuna el Gebel on prehistoric Egypt. No permanent job was available at the time and she was not in a position to move round the country, so she decided to train as accountant and she started to write. As her books began to sell, she gave up accountancy and taught part-time in Egyptology at Liverpool, sometimes as a locum when someone was on sabbatical for instance. As an honorary fellow there she continues to supervise dissertations.

Her present job description is still being worked out. The KNH end involves doing all the tutoring for the distance learning course and should the Taught Course resume, she would probably do most of the teaching. As Tutor and Administrator of the Distance Learning Egyptology Certificate Course, she is busy redeveloping all the teaching materials for it, which is a huge task. She is the author of many books including 'Hatschepsut' and 'Cleopatra', and with her husband, she runs The Rutherford Press, which produces books on Egyptology and ploughs the profits into Egyptian fieldwork. Some money has been given to the EES to be used for excavations in the Delta and there has been a donation to the Museum for the new gallery. At the Manchester Museum she organizes regular lectures on Egyptological topics. Besides all this, she lectures to adult classes and groups from time to time. In common with many of those working in Egyptology in Manchester, Joyce is keen to say how much she owes to Rosalie David.[3]

The third member of Rosalie David's staff is Ryan Metcalfe. His background in both chemistry and bio-molecular science fit him perfectly for the kind of work in which the KNH Centre specializes. In the course of his MSc research he looked into disease in ancient lung tissue but switched his focus for his PhD. His interest was in the preservation of protein in human tissue. In order to find out more, he looked at the mummification of mice using a form of natron assembled in the laboratory. He was able to demonstrate that there is no evidence of enzyme degradation as the cell nuclei and the tissue structure remain perfect. In his post-doctoral phase, funded by the Leverhulme Trust, he began to look into the preservation of plants and their DNA. He has been a Teaching Fellow since 2008 and lectures on molecular biology, ancient DNA and protein analysis.

A variety of methods can test the DNA and the chemical composition of plants. This can help to identify where the plants originated and can assist the investigation into trade routes. Egypt has a large number of species which are found nowhere else, making it an important area for both research and experiment. These studies may be based on plant material or pollens which are very sturdy. As part of his studies, Dr Metcalfe has attempted to test the survival of DNA using one of the prescriptions in the Ebers Medical Papyrus. Using pigskin as the nearest available substitute for human skin, a substance was smeared on and left for varying lengths of time. The samples were then tested to

---

[3] Tyldesley, Joyce 2008

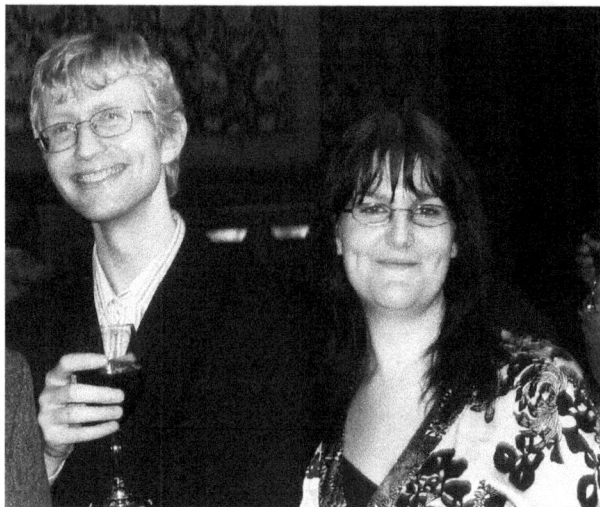

Fig.56 Ryan Metcalfe and Jenefer Cockitt

evaluate how far DNA was transferred between the skin and the ointment. [4]

Other studies carried out by post-graduate researchers in recent years have looked at various aspects of DNA. One study by Parker in 2003 was able to confirm that a cat's head in the Museum, which had been visually identified as *felis sylvestris* because of its large size was, in fact, a representative of that species. Another study, by Bibby in 2005, established the gender of one of the human mummies. The Two Brothers again came under scrutiny with a view to establishing their actual relationship. The results showed that it is 185 times more likely that they are related than that they are not. It is hoped that future studies will require smaller and smaller samples, a factor which might allow replication of experiments, and that sterile facilities will reduce the risk of contamination. [5]

Besides the staff members there are a number of associates of the KNH Centre. The professional teams which support the work of the Centre are a mixture of those who are currently studying for further degrees, have graduated from courses run there, or are already working in the University or hospital.

Dr Jenefer Cockitt is a Research Associate with a background in ancient history and archaeology. She came to the KNH Centre to do an MSc. As a fairly local schoolgirl, she confesses to a childhood fascination with the toes of the mummies in the Manchester Museum. Her main focus is radio carbon dates which were obtained many years ago. This technique has improved over the last four decades meaning that some adjustment is necessary. Carbon dating was carried out on the material obtained during the unwrapping of Mummy 1770. For her Master's dissertation, Cockitt looked at the results of dating studies carried out on these samples during the 1970s and 1980s and came to the conclusion that contamination by resins

and other material could have distorted the results, making the mummy seem older than it really is. Following on from this, her doctoral thesis aimed at testing her hypothesis that the accepted chronology of ancient Egypt, as presented by carbon 14 dating, was quite inaccurate. She looked at results from other areas and concluded that for some, such as Britain, results were acceptable, while Egyptian ones were wildly out. The next step was to explore why this should be. Much material found in Egyptian tombs, by far the most common source of samples used for testing, was re-used in ancient times. Many examples of this can be proved. Typical are the Leicester Mummies. These two, from Akhmin, appear from their coffins to date from the XXVth Dynasty but study of the human remains give a much later, XXIXth Dynasty date. The re-use of funerary equipment reflects an environment in which raw materials were scarce, so that nothing was allowed to go to waste. Another reason for the distortion of dates is due to the common use of resins and bitumen in funerary practice. [6]

The Centre taps into the expertise of many associate professionals. Judith Adams for example is a Clinical Radiologist working in the hospital. She has been involved with all the recent studies of human remains using the most up to date equipment and methods. She has used computed tomography to study mummies slice by slice. Now that non-invasive methods are the order of the day, this work is crucial to the extension of knowledge. In her article in the latest scientific report from the Centre, she points out that MRI and ultrasound scans are of no help when looking into ancient remains since they need water in the tissues if they are to work. The three dimensional filmless records which can now be made, can be transferred onto DVD for storage. This information can also be used to guide scientists to areas suitable for biopsies. [7]

David Counsell works full-time as Consultant Anaesthetist at Maelor Hospital, Wrexham, but he finds time to be an Honorary Research Associate in the KNH Centre in the field of paleopharmacology. He was born in Bolton and had the advantage of access to its major collection of Egyptian artefacts. He believes that this was the source of his early interest but he never saw it as a possible career path. Instead, he went to Leicester University to read Medicine then specialized in anaesthesia. As a consultant in Blackpool he was mainly concerned with cardio-thoracic surgery. His work entailed many exams and much study but he decided to learn something different. He applied to do the Manchester Certificate course but was unable to get on to it immediately. Instead he attended a series of lectures being held in Blackpool. This confirmed his interest and he joined the certificate group in 1993. While he was doing the course a television programme was made about the alleged presence of cocaine on Egyptian mummies. Rosalie David took part in this and Counsell's interest was aroused.

---

[4] Metcalfe, Ryan 2010
[5] David, Rosalie (ed) 2008

[6] Cockitt, Jenefer 2010
[7] Adams, Judith, in David, Rosalie (ed) 2008

Shortly afterwards, Rosalie asked him if he could help in the analysis of residues found in base-ring ware. These pots, made in Cyprus, were thought to be shaped like opium poppy pods so the suggestion was that they had been used in the opium trade. The residues, scraped out of these pots, were analysed to try to detect the presence of alkaloids. Subsequently he has taken part in TV programmes such as 'The Private Lives of the Pharaohs' in which the blue lotus was examined for its narcotic and aphrodisiac effects. None were found, although the programme tried to suggest otherwise. David's PhD thesis, finished in 2006, was on the subject of 'Intoxicants in Ancient Egypt'. He has looked into the possible presence of cocaine and nicotine in mummies and has explored the possibility of contamination of specimens. Since he began his work, there have been two major developments in the research undertaken by the KNH Centre. The whole area of ancient pharmacology is being explored and the methods of analysis have developed significantly. David continues to lecture and to publish articles in such respected organs as the Journal of the Royal Society of Medicine, while still working full-time at the Wrexham Hospital.[8]

By his own admission John Denton started as a complete failure at school, left at 15 and took up a job as a technician at a teacher training college. Eventually he moved into hospital work and remembers that he was present when the Mummy Team unwrapped the first mummy. He was working as a technician in the hospital when someone said, 'do you fancy coming downstairs to see what they're doing there?' He knew the pathologists involved and so he tucked himself away at the side while they took all the pictures. Since then he has become more and more involved though he says very definitely that he is not an Egyptologist. At first he did not know Rosalie David personally but he had read about her work. In 1998 he began to give talks about modern histological techniques to MSc students who were specialising in ancient Egypt. He was approached by Rosalie David directly the next year and he gave half hour talks on a purely voluntary basis. There are a lot of people working in that way but according to Denton, 'there's a reason for that, call it charisma or whatever, she has a way of getting you to do something and using your talents.' About seven years ago he started doing more and more, taking on a number of students each year. He gives two day talks, then splits the students up for half-day practical sessions. He says, 'we get a lot of tissue from our patients and we can use it (with their consent). Manchester Royal Infirmary is a regional centre and we get soft tissue samples from all over the country and Scotland too.' He has become very interested in the process of mummification and would love to try it out on human beings. Some people have offered their bodies for experiment but legislation is against it. Bob Brier was able to use a real body for such an experiment in America but in Britain it was not allowed because as soon as bodies are mummified, they have to be cremated or buried which negates the whole experiment. This means that they are restricted to using small samples

[8] Counsell, David2009

Fig. 57 John Denton

for histology, and other methods, such as laser ablation mass spectometry (LAMS).

One interesting experiment on some tissues cultured from mummies, resulted in the finding of *aspergillus niger* a pathogenic material which lodges in the lungs, and dry rot fungus. In a programme for National Geographic Channel, Rosalie and Denton (slightly tongue in cheek) played up the question of whether this could have been what Lord Carnarvon picked up from the tombs. Denton is very aware of the problems and pitfalls involved in the study of ancient tissue. He believes that any sort of study should be treated like a scene of crime. The researchers should always be gowned up like surgeons. One major problem is that all the material has been contaminated with other DNA since understanding of this is so relatively recent. One has only to look at old photographs of people leaning over mummies and touching remains with bare hands to see that this is true. Another problem also relates to how samples have been handled in the past. Denton says, 'all modern techniques can be wrong if the samples are mislabelled. Histology provides the screener. I had one labelled *pleura*; when it was hydrated it turned out to be a flower which we think was perhaps part of a wreath or garland put on at the time of the funeral, interesting in itself.'

Denton is interested in metals as well. Renal patients have problems with their chemistry. If someone has too much phosphorus, the parathyroid tries to counteract it. He shares equipment with Alan Cox, a metal expert and they do measurements on urine to test for metals. UV rays are used to burn samples; the smoke which comes off is passed through various stages and ends at a mass spectrometer. They can measure quantities down to parts per million. He is enthusiastic about this precision and points out that new technologies drive this on and aspects of it can be applied to ancient material.[9]

Following the long tradition of interest in the dental health of the ancient Egyptians which was the cause of so much trouble to them, in many cases fatally, Roger Forshaw, a dentist who took early retirement in 2000, now works at the KNH Centre as a research associate. He was a Leeds graduate and spent most of his working life in Yorkshire. He had no background in Egyptology before this, only a general interest in history. With more time on his hands he came across a book on ancient Egypt which captured his attention and he began to read up on the subject. This led to his taking a certificate course in Egyptology, not the Manchester one in this instance, but that provided on-line by the University of Exeter. He took a particular interest in hieroglyphics and did several courses with Pam Scott and Penny Wilson. He used to go up to Durham for practice in reading hieroglyphs. When he decided to do an MSc full-time he had to live in Manchester for six months, where he did some research on the Elliot Smith collection of skulls for his dissertation. He did not confine himself to the dental state of the individuals but rather studied the characteristics of the skulls themselves. Having completed this, he inherited the mantle of Judith Miller, a professional dentist who had been teaching the module on teeth to the MSc students. She had to retire through ill-health and Roger happened to be in the right place at the right time. He now does the teaching and the marking for that course whilst pursuing his research into the Nubian skulls. He has used the Manchester samples as well as the Duckworth collection in Cambridge where they have a huge number of specimens. He has worked with Angelique Courthals who is no longer at the KNH Centre but they have collaborated on several articles, one of which is about to appear in the American Journal.[10]

Jacqueline Campbell until recently was a Post-doctoral Researcher in the KNH Centre. She originally came from Leeds, and studied biochemistry at Nottingham University. She became a graduate trainee with the CWS in Manchester and worked for them for seventeen years. Having been made redundant in 1988, she set up her own business which involved retail marketing and franchising. She did some consultancy work and a lot for the Arts Council as vice-chair for the Octagon Theatre in Bolton. This had taken her, a scientist and businesswoman, into the world of arts and history and she loved it. A chance encounter with a neighbour of hers, Rosalie David, led to a conversation which resulted in her applying for a further degree. That conversation changed Jackie's life and she feels that it was fate that Rosalie came into her shop that day. Before this Jackie had no connection with Egyptology although an old friend who had been consultant psychiatrist at a local

hospital gave her his entire collection of Classical and Egyptological books when he became unwell. That was when she first picked up a book by Rosalie David.

She began the MSc course in 2002 opting to look at the prescriptions in the Egyptian medical papyri to see if they had any efficacy, concentrating mainly on the Ebers Papyrus. She evaluated the written prescriptions and compared their content to modern pharmaceutical protocols. Her husband is a pharmacist so she had always had an interest in pharmacy as well as horticulture. After this she decided to study for a PhD, testing the reliability of the written word in a more practical way. She wanted to find out whether these plants existed and whether they worked as the texts suggested. It took her back to her original degree in biochemistry, which had been based in the faculty of Agriculture at Nottingham. The Petrie Museum in London and the British Museum had given many of their plants to Kew where they allowed her to examine their ancient Egyptian collection of five hundred plants. At a time when it was difficult to access local resources, the British Museum allowed her to look at their whole collection which no-one has really studied since Sir Percy Newberry. Stephen Quirke gave her access to the Petrie collection. More recently she was able to work with the fantastic herbarium at Manchester Museum presided over by Leander Wolstenholme who curates a million plant specimens all donated by the cotton manufacturers of Manchester, which include a wonderful collection of Egyptian plants.

Again, through contacts of Rosalie, the Cairo Museum allowed her access to their collection of plants, much of which was from the Tutankhamun assemblage. Some of the material is unprovenanced so it is impossible to know whether it had been carried into a tomb by accident or by some burrowing animal. It is important to find out whether and how the plants could have grown in Egypt. Received wisdom in an academic world dominated by classical ideas has always claimed that the Greeks were the first to develop useful medical and viable pharmacological knowledge. Dr Campbell, working with Professor Mohamed el Demerdash hoped to produce results to alter that perception. This project which is being carried out in partnership with the NRC in Cairo, the University of Cairo, the South Sinai Environmental Agency, in association with a number of museums and academic institutions, has complex aims. Earlier research has looked closely at the papyri or it has looked at the botanical evidence. The problem of identification of plants mentioned in the papyri is central to the study since there have been differing translations of plant names over the years. What is quite clear is that the project has huge significance and importance in modern Egypt where local people, especially the women, are working to grow those plants which are thought to have been known in ancient times. It is hoped that this production of pharmaceutical plants will bring in profits for the community. Plants from wild stock can accumulate higher concentrations of active ingredients, according to the stress produced by environmental factors

[9] Denton, John2008
[10] Forshaw, Roger2009

Fig. 58 Jacqueline Campbell with some of her plant specimens

such as drought, high temperatures, soil salinity and other environmental conditions which Egypt provides in abundance. The local Bedouin healers are being consulted and recent folk medicine practices studied. According to Professor Demerdash, it is vital to document and conserve traditional knowledge of medicinal plants and to identify those plants which are globally significant. A plant gene bank has been set up to preserve Egyptian species for future generations.

The Sinai research came about when Rosalie mentioned the pharmacy project to Tony Taylor, a man who has extensive contacts in Egypt. He said 'I met a man called Mohamed el Demerdash who is growing medicinal plants. I think he'd like to meet you'. So two years ago, before Jackie began her PhD, he brought Demerdash to the hotel where they were all staying on one of their workshop visits to Cairo. There was an immediate rapport and Rosalie made him part of the research team instantaneously. Dr Demerdash has been a key part of the project, growing the medicinal plants of ancient Egypt while Jackie was producing them in this country. The Centre was granted a Leverhulme award for work on botanical and medical science which funded her research. She feels very proud to have been able to contribute and has now completed her two year placement.

She has many happy memories including one from her last visit to a Bedouin Healer in Sinai, not in a tent, but in one of the concrete huts they have now. They all sat on the floor but she could not get up because her knee had locked. Two of them hoisted her up. Then the Healer told her to put something on her knee. When she asked what it was he said 'it's colocynth oil'. This is a substance which is pharmaceutically a very aggressive purgative. Jackie had never come across it being used as a topical application, but when she looked at the sources she found one reference to its being applied externally in ancient

Egypt. As she left, he also gave her a little bag saying, 'you must take this back with you'. When she asked what it was, she was told, 'nature's pharmacy'. When she commented that it looked remarkably like animal dung, she was told that it was donkey dung, but not just from any donkey. These donkeys, which live in the mountains, eat medicinal plants exclusively.   He said, 'much of what they eat is excreted and I make it into a tea which is good for stomach complaints and the digestion'. It is also used topically to treat wounds. When Jackie checked her records, she found remedies using boiled up dung for topical use. These were remedies she had assumed to be fanciful, but this experience taught her that there might be something in them after all.[11]

Recently graduated PhD, Jacky Finch, has been engaged in a fascinating project concerning the possible early development of prosthetic medicine in ancient Egypt. Her studies focus on two examples of false big toes. One, known as the Greville Chester Great Toe is made from cartonnage (glue and linen) and shows distinct signs of having been worn. It is on display in the British Museum. The other, a complex three component model in wood and leather is in the Egyptian Museum, Cairo. Both examples are thought to come from the late New Kingdom or early Third Intermediate Period and both appear to have been laced onto the foot using a series of holes. The research was trying to prove the efficacy of both these artefacts. The question is whether these have indeed been worn, either purely as cosmetic replacements perhaps of some religious significance, or as functional prostheses to help the person walk. Unable to test the actual objects, amputees were invited to volunteer to wear and test exact design copies under laboratory conditions. Such research using human subjects was challenging and involved applying for Research Ethics permission before any work could

---

[11] Campbell, Jacqueline 2007

Fig. 59 Professor Mohammed el
Demerdash

Fig. 60 Jacky Finch at the Pharmacy
and Medicine Conference

be started. Sourcing materials and getting to grips with methods of construction came next, then replicas were made of each artefact to fit the volunteers selected.

Jacky has been extremely fortunate to receive most generous assistance from Dr Glyn Heath, Department of Prosthetics and Orthotics at the University of Salford. The testing of the replicas was carried out at their Centre for Rehabilitation and Human Performance Research (CRHPR) Gait Laboratory using state of the art optoelectronic motion analysis. This project has attracted media attention as have several of the Centre's researches proving the continued public fascination with all things ancient Egyptian. Over ninety articles appeared in the press to attract volunteers to come forward, one with the dreadful punning headline, 'Call me Toe-tankhamun!' Dr Andreas Nerlich, the German paleopathologist, lecturing to the Pharmacy and Medicine Symposium in 2008 in Manchester, detailed his work on the female mummy whom he found wearing the 'toe prosthesis' now in the Egyptian Museum. Jacky was able to update him with her research on the functionality of the artefact that he had found in 1998.[12]

She had first become fascinated by ancient Egypt when, as a B.Ed student she saw the Tutankhamun Exhibition at the British museum in 1972. This fired her enthusiasm and, while teaching Biological Sciences over the next twenty eight years, she was also reading widely and attending courses on the subject. She was able eventually to visit Egypt in 1999. Having taken early retirement

she was at last at liberty to develop her interest fully and enrolled on the certificate course at Manchester University which started in 2000. Having made a study of Egyptian proctology and purges for her dissertation, in common with many other students on this course, she found that she had an urge to continue with academic study. This led her to join the MSc course in Bio-medical and Forensic Studies in Egyptology in the KNH Centre, though not without some trepidation. It was over thirty years since her last academic exams and there were practical considerations too since it would involve considerable travel. She did not allow this to affect her decision however and her studies proved a great success. She made a special study of the deformed and restored mummified arm of a body in the Oriental Museum in Durham and was allowed to bring it to Manchester for study by CT scan and radiography in the Department of Imaging Science and Biomedical Engineering at the Manchester Royal Infirmary. Thus she was able to be fully involved in the multi-disciplinary methods of the KNH Centre. During her PhD research she has been privileged to work in the British Museum and, most notably, in the Cairo Museum store. She expresses gratitude to all those who helped to make these opportunities possible: Dr Maghdy El Ghandour of the Supreme Council of Antiquities and Dr Wafaa El Saddik of the Cairo Museum granted her permission to work in Egypt while Dr John Taylor of the British Museum gave her special access to materials in London. She points out that her path was also eased by Professor David, who as always, provided help and encouragement throughout.

Like Jackie Campbell, Natalie Mc Creesh, who has now completed her PhD research, looked into ancient remedies

---

[12] Finch, Jacqueline, 2008

Fig.61 Detail from the tomb of Nebamun

Fig.62 Natalie McCreesh checking out wax cones and the blue lotus

which are recorded in the Ebers Papyrus. She is particularly interested in hair. Typical of the researchers in the Centre, she has used a wide range of scientific methods and combined these with study of the other sources of evidence. Studies of hair under scanning electron microscopes reveal damage to hair as well as the remains of lice. One study of mummies from the Dahkleh Oasis shows evidence of severe damage to hair including skin scaling and lesions, possibly caused by an inherited condition. A condition referred to in the Ebers Medical Papyrus as 'swelling of the hair' may refer to a cyst and the treatment recommended is the knife. Studies of the substances recommended in the papyrus reveal the use of emollients and herbs many of which may have helped, though the treatment of grey hair with dark coloured ingredients may smack of sympathetic magic. Although many of the treatments were of rational origin, perhaps the recipe for making an enemy's hair fall out was not quite so sound. Natalie is typical of many students here, in that she is creative in her methods. One of the questions she wanted to investigate for her master's thesis was whether the cones which are depicted on the heads of people in wall-paintings, often in scenes of feasting, were made of perfumed oils or unguents as many scholars suggest .

Natalie devised her own recipe for such cones using lard and essential oils in order to see whether they would melt during feasting. This experiment could then be linked to analysis of ancient hair to try to identify the use of such perfumed substances. Her long-suffering family became her guinea pigs and patiently sat with these objects on their heads in a tropical temperature achieved by turning the central heating up to maximum

Now, with her doctor's thesis finished, she has looked into a whole range of fats, oils and resins and was, in 2008, involved in the investigation of the mummy of Takabuti,

which has a fine head of apparently auburn curls. She has also carried out tests on the black coating of a coffin in Cairo. Despite some problems in acquiring samples, she was able to investigate whether it was a black resin or some kind of varnish and whether it was made of bitumen or pitch. She has been able to use a variety of methods including gas chromatography mass spectrometry (GCMS) which shows up what substances are present in the sample.[13]

Using similar analytical techniques, Dr Judith Seath is working on ancient resins and unguents from the pre- and early dynastic periods to discover their composition. The substances used were plant material such as resins, minerals, asphalt and animal products like beeswax. The plant products are most common and may originate from such plants as acacia, pistachio and myrrh. This may indicate active trade in plants from outside Egypt. It is known that Queen Hatshepsut sent an expedition to the land of Punt to bring back incense trees and the remains of these have been identified at Deir el Bahri.

Curiously, Hatshepsut herself has come under the scrutiny of a KNH researcher. DNA was an important aspect of the work of a former member of the KNH Centre, Angelique Courthals, who has now moved abroad to continue her work. In November 2007 in a talk to the Manchester Branch of the EES she outlined some of the studies which have been made of the Royal mummies. Like many of

---

[13] McCreesh, Natalie 2009

her colleagues she has had experience of the world of television. While working on the royal DNA she was filmed at work. It was very difficult for her to carry out her experiments since a camera man was crawling round under her arms trying to get the best picture. The film involves the study of the newly identified mummy of Queen Hatshepsut whose tooth was discovered in a casket and found to fit exactly into a hole in the jaw of an unidentified body, that found in a tomb numbered KV 60A. DNA studies on this mummy could have enormous potential in solving some of the mysteries of Egyptian history. A study of four female mummies, including this one, was carried out with the permission of the Egyptian authorities in order to study their DNA and to try to find a connection with Hatshepsut. They were all scanned using equipment loaned by Siemens. There was similar equipment available in the Museum in Cairo but because it had been donated by National Geographic TV Channel and the work was being filmed by Discovery Channel, they were not allowed to use it. Sadly this seems to illustrate that TV's priorities may not always be purely aimed at scientific discoveries. Despite these obstacles, the outcome of the work was positive. The mummy identified as Queen Hatshepsut was also shown through mitochondrial DNA to be related to Queen Ahmose Nefertari who was her great grandmother. The study also suggested some of the health problems from which she may have suffered, which included diabetes, osteoporosis, bone cancer and tooth abscesses.[14]

Fig.63 Karen Exell with some of her charges

Although not a part of the KNH team itself, the story would be incomplete without covering the current situation in the Manchester Museum, which now works closely with the KNH Centre. The Curator of Egypt and the Sudan, Karen Exell has a new vision for the collection. She is about to embark upon a radical redesign of the Egyptian Gallery which, together with the Mediterranean Gallery, is scheduled to be re-opened in 2012, exactly a century after the opening of the Jesse Haworth extension. This project as always is dependent on funding but, if it goes ahead as planned it will be an exciting time in the Museum.

Karen studied Egyptology at Oxford, specializing in the language of ancient Egypt. After graduating she was drawn towards Museum Studies and for a time worked with John Prag as a volunteer at Manchester Museum. She then did an MA in Museum Studies at St Andrews before going to London for a further two years. She worked for the Institute of Archaeology doing such things as scanning papyri for the Petrie Museum in University College London. She went north to take up a position as Deputy Curator in Durham Museum. While there, she did a PhD on the subject of Ramesside votive stelae, which she completed in 2006. After a spell working in London for the EES, of which she is a trustee, she was appointed to her position in Manchester. Now she is very busy both behind the scenes, cataloguing and reorganising parts of the collection, and also in the public eye, giving lectures, working with primary learning groups and liaising with

other colleagues. She is Chair of ACCES which is a Specialist Network for those working with collections from Egypt and the Sudan in Museums. She has also found time to publish a new reading of Ramesside period votive stelae entitled 'Soldiers, Sailors and Sandalmakers.'[15]

[14] Courthals, Angelique 2008

[15] Exell, Karen, 2010

19. Three days in the life of the KNH Centre

It is September 2008, a rain-swept Monday morning in Manchester University. An international symposium entitled 'Pharmacy and Medicine in Ancient Egypt' is about to commence. It is taking place under the auspices of the KNH Centre for Bio-medical Egyptology. The programme for this event encapsulates the range and interest of the typical work of the centre and it also contains some pointers to the future. The conference delegates come from all over the world and it seems particularly fitting that a substantial delegation comes from Egypt. All are eagerly awaiting a varied programme of presentations, some from researchers working at the KNH centre itself, others given by Egyptian scholars and academics, representatives from Hungary, Romania, Germany and Italy, as well as members of other British universities and even an independent scholar. The audience is similarly varied.

Sitting at the front are the prime movers, Professor Rosalie David, Professor Moushira Erfan Zaki and the eponymous KNH herself. Their contributions set the scene for the whole event. Professor David opens the proceedings with a summary of the aims of the Manchester Pharmacy in Egyptology Project which is backed by a grant from the Leverhulme Trust. The research plan entails assessment of the role and efficacy of pharmacy in ancient Egypt, a re-evaluation of the written sources, an investigation into how far there were magical elements in Egyptian medicine and an investigation into how far it predates Greek medical practice. Using a wide variety of methods including DNA, it is hoped to compile a more complete Egyptian Pharmacopeia. As the KNH Centre is working with the National Research Centre in Cairo, Professor Moushira Erfan Zaki from the centre explains its work. The NRC is mainly engaged in research relating to many aspects of life in modern Egypt, such as water desalinisation, medical provision and the development of technology. The Professor's presence at this conference illustrates how seriously the work of the KNH Centre is taken by the Egyptian authorities. She explains that one major part of her centre's work is the development of international links.

As the title of the event suggests, many of the presentations deal with aspects of pharmacy, especially the questions relating to the validity of ancient Egyptian knowledge. Much of the work of the centre revolves around the study of mummy tissues and skeletal remains held in the Manchester Collection. Many researchers are attempting to explain both disease and its treatment using examples from the collection. Mervyn Harris gives a paper on surviving head injuries. He has been studying a skull from Grafton Elliott Smith's collection of bones from Nubia, which clearly shows that its owner had suffered severe injuries on more than one occasion; at least one of which healed completely while others had begun to improve

*Fig. 64 Dr Moushira Erfan Zaki
at the Manchester Conference*

before the individual's death. This paper is backed up by a guest speaker from Germany, Andreas Nerlich who has found similar evidence in several individuals. One of his examples is a female mummy which shows clear evidence of a successful amputation of a big toe. Other studies of bone reveal information about diet and nutrition.

A gathering like this is not all sitting and listening. One of the most important aspects is to meet with colleagues, to share ideas and to forge links of friendship and co-operation which can be built upon in the future. An official reception at Manchester Town Hall, where the Lord Mayor of Manchester (actually a lady) welcomed all the delegates to the city, indicates the regard in which the KNH centre and its work are held by the City. So often it is one's own who do not appreciate what one has achieved. On the last night, a Conference dinner at Manchester's Midland Hotel sets the seal on the event. Perhaps the most important long-term outcome is the agreement of the delegates to the idea of a Professional Society for Mummy Studies to be centred upon the KNH Centre in Manchester. This is intended to be an international body with a guiding committee from a wide range of countries. Egypt of course will be involved as will Canada, Italy, France, and Great Britain. It will have a responsibility to publish specialised papers, to hold regular workshops and symposia and eventually possibly to offer bursaries. Before this conference ends, it is known that the University of Manchester are happy to agree and that the next symposium will take place in Aswan the following year.

20. Investigating Takabuti

It is May 23rd, 2008 and a BBC team is filming a documentary about the Ulster Museum in Belfast so the Museum staff have brought their one precious mummy over to Manchester for study by the Mummy Team. Present on this bank holiday Friday at the KNH, besides Professor David and the team from Belfast, are John Denton, the histology expert and Ken Wildsmith, the endoscopy king. Watching from the sidelines is an assortment of PhD and MSc students all engaged in a wide variety of research projects including osteology, ancient tumours and Egyptian prosthetics. In the centre of the laboratory is a large wooden box, still closed. The Manchester team does not know exactly what to expect when the box is opened, though it is known to contain the mummy of an Egyptian lady of high rank named Takabuti.

The preparations for filming take some time as the lights are positioned to avoid shadows and the members of the company to be filmed are lined up round the box in order of height with the Professor standing at the far end to get the best view. The director asks for silence and explains what he wants. 'Rosalie, this is your bit. I'd like you to tell the group just what it is you see. Talk in your own words and tell the people what you see about Takabuti. Feel free to say something to the next person if it strikes you. It should be free-flowing.' The film crew are counted in and Rosalie says, 'This is such a well preserved mummy. It's probably because of the resin which was used. The hair of course is incredibly well preserved. It's very unusual to see all this hair as they usually shaved the heads after death. I'm very excited to see whether she's a natural redhead or whether it's dyed with henna which they sometimes did. We can probably find out with tests.' She comments further that redheads were very special in Egypt and that this might explain the retention of the hair. 'The eye sockets have been packed with rolls of linen. This was often done and we may be able to detect the remains of the eyes behind them.' One PhD student observing is interested in this as her speciality is ancient Egyptian prosthetics. Another is excited by the hair. The beautifully preserved head even retains the eyelids.

John Denton is introduced to the camera. He also comments on the state of preservation of the mummy and asks whether there's a chance of endoscopy. The Belfast team explain that the sternum had collapsed when the mummy was unwrapped in 1835 and this might provide an entry point. The mummy was rewrapped in the original bandages however, so it may prove inaccessible. The lady is wrapped from neck to ankle, with an elegant right arm lying in a straight position outside the bandages. Her nails are manicured indicating a comfortable life-style. Her shoulders and upper chest are covered with a mesh of blue

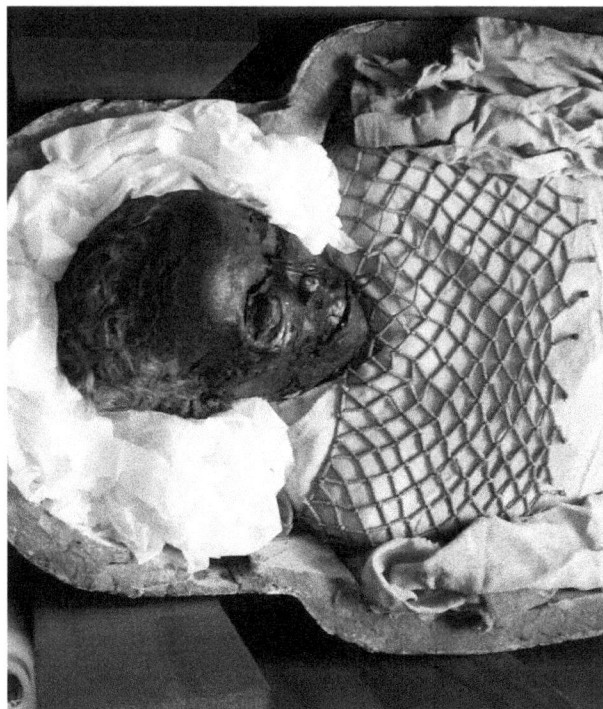

Fig. 65 Takabuti on her trip to Manchester

faience beads. She lies in her own coffin which Rosalie believes might have been made to measure as it is such a good fit. The outside is painted, though the observers cannot study the inscriptions while the coffin lies in its travelling box. The Belfast Museum has the lid but has not brought it to Manchester. Takabuti probably dates to about 660BC, the XXVth Dynasty when mummification techniques were at their peak. The flow of information, delivered instantaneously and unseen is apparently completely effortless, reflecting the speaker's great talent for communication. Now, after this preliminary survey, the body will be taken to Manchester Royal Infirmary for the more technical tests including CT scans and endoscopy.

The scientific investigation was begun the day after the events described above and the process was filmed by the BBC. The resulting programme was shown in October 2009 and included coverage of the wide variety of methods used to study Takabuti, not only in Manchester, but also in Dundee, Cardiff and, of course, Belfast.[1] The mummy had already been the subject of a 3D laser scan at Queens University but had come to Manchester for a full body CT scan. The ancient patient was taken up the road to Manchester Royal Infirmary. Preliminary reports suggested a generally healthy individual whose age

---

[1] Borderline Productions, 2009

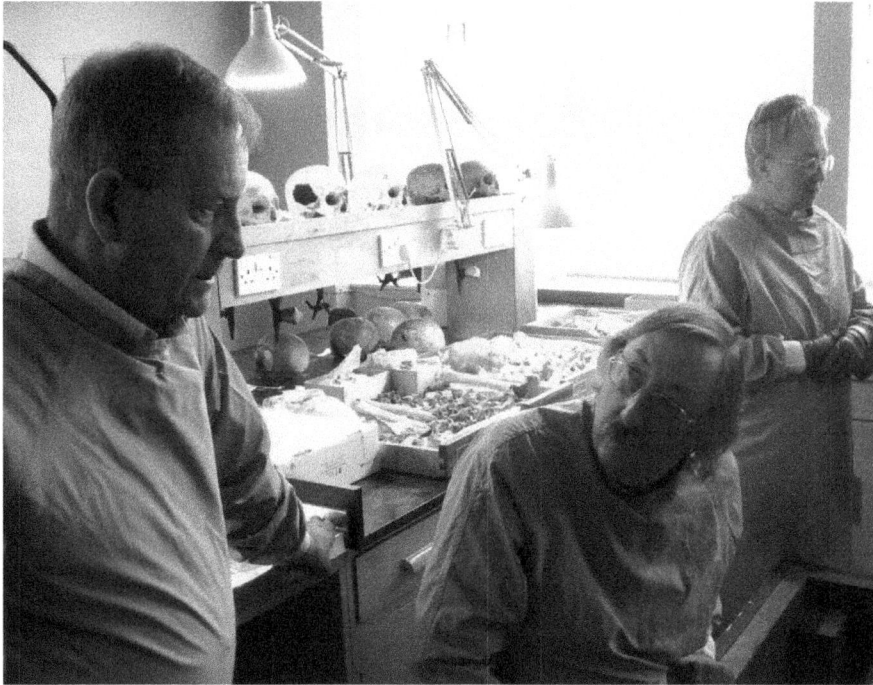

Fig.66 Ken Wildsmith and John Denton await the filming of Takabuti

and cause of death still needed to be decided. The scan revealed a mysterious package inside the upper left region of the torso. Unusually in mummified remains, the brain appeared to have been left in place but the heart, which was normally left in situ, appeared to be missing.

The next phase of investigation was an endoscopic exploration. Ken Wildsmith who has been with the Mummy Team since the 1970s was able to use the latest methods to harvest samples from inside the body through a hole in the chest. These could then be studied under the microscope. John Denton, Senior Research Fellow at the KNH Centre was in charge of this. Disappointingly, the samples proved to be contaminated with wood sawdust which had been employed in the mummification process. This meant little human tissue could be detected in the samples but instead there was strong evidence of parasitic infestation. The *taraphagus* mite which lives on wood had made itself at home, used the sawdust packing of the mummy as food, and left behind its faeces.

One of the most dramatic features of Takabuti was her apparently orange hair. Heads were normally shaved prior to embalming, but for some reason hers had been left. Not only this, it had been carefully curled using hot tongs. From the original accounts of the unwrapping in 1835, it is known that the hair was in an excellent condition and state of preservation immediately after the unwrapping. It was reported to be very fine, about three and a half inches long, forming ringlets, and was of a deep auburn shade. A lock of her hair was taken at the time of unwrapping, tied with a ribbon and kept in a little box. This lock still retains the auburn colour, but the hair on Takabuti's head is now yellow-orange and very dry. Her hair in general was not well preserved; it was coated in fungal matter and

debris, and had become weak, breaking easily. Some of it was covered with a coating, and this was well preserved. This indicated that the coating had offered some protection to the hair, a finding seen in other samples studied. The appearance of the coating was like oil or fat. Cross sections of the hair showed it to be Caucasian. The hair had been cut relatively close to the time of death or post-mortem. The hair was set into neat artificial curls but the curl would not have held that position for very long without some form of aid. It is possible that the residue on the hair (identified microscopically as a smooth coating over the hair), may have been applied like a hair-gel, to hold the style in place. [2]

The film made for BBC Northern Ireland followed the investigation into Takabuti to its end. In order to get a feel for the kind of life she may have led, the cameras followed Winifred Glover of the Ulster Museum in Belfast and Rosalie David from Manchester, to Egypt where they were given privileged access to the tomb of Nefer which contains one of the oldest mummies found. Their host, Dr Zahi Hawass, Secretary General of the Supreme Council for Antiquities, also allowed them access to mummies not normally on display.

The film also followed the process of reconstructing the face of Takabuti. After the face of the mummy had been scanned in detail by Cardiff University the data was handed over to Caroline Wilkinson, formerly in Manchester and now in Dundee, who was responsible for the final portrait. The result was the climax of the film in much the same way as the first such example, the head of Mummy 1770 in Manchester, had been in the 1970s.

---

[2] McCreesh, Natalie 2010

21. From amateur to academe

Manchester has always had a strong tradition of interest in Egyptology. In earlier times the main drive came from academics and those of some wealth and social influence. Since the early 1970s it has become the centre of a great popular movement. Rosalie David's passion for promoting knowledge of Egyptology led her to develop a course which would provide inspiration for successive generations of students. This took the form of a series of lectures given by Doctor (as she was then) David as well as some serious written work and studies in Hieroglyphics. It was aimed at the achievement of a Certificate in Egyptology. The course was originally located in the Extramural Department of the University and, after successive changes in the organisation of that department it is currently running in the KNH Centre for Biomedical Egyptology in the Faculty of Life Sciences. Keeping up with the tradition of using the latest methods in all aspects of Egyptology, the course is now studied on-line by distance learning.

Over the years it has attracted a wide range of people from all kinds of backgrounds and it has produced many students who have developed from enthusiastic amateurs, in some cases with little or no knowledge at the outset, into professional Egyptologists. There have also been many who have become involved actively in the Museum and locally based research. The popularity of the course has been such that it has been said jokingly that at any dinner party in South Manchester at least one guest would have done the certificate course. This may be a great exaggeration but there is no doubt that the course has changed the lives of many people.

The course brought together people with a common interest and one of the most important aspects for many participants was meeting fellow enthusiasts. Over the years students sometimes went on interesting visits abroad, to Egypt or to other places where there were important collections of material. They also attended lectures which were given under the auspices of the Egypt Exploration Society (EES). These lectures formed part of the taught Certificate course but were open to EES members and guests too. Lectures covered a wide range of subjects, many concerned with the work of the EES in Egypt. These lectures were organised by the 'Northern Branch' of the EES. Lectures and events by the EES are now under the heading of 'EES North' and meetings will not only be based in Manchester.

There were however those who did not want to be part of the academic world but who were nevertheless very interested in ancient Egypt. For some of these people the EES was seen as too academic. There was clearly a need for a society which covered more general subjects so the 'Amateur Ancient Egypt Society' was formed. The constitution of that Society originally specifically excluded any professional Egyptologists from involvement. It met in the Portico Library which only held about twenty five people at a time. Most of the lectures were given by members and some of these, like Bob Partridge and Victor Blunden, went on to become professional lecturers. The MAES was the first of what is now a large number of regional Egyptology Societies in the UK. It is now large enough to need a full–sized lecture theatre to accommodate its regular meetings at the Manchester Conference Centre.

When Bob Partridge finished the certificate course he and a number of his fellow-students joined the Society. There was a substantial hole in people's lives when they finished the course so Bob and about twelve others joined en masse, increasing the membership considerably. Societies evolve and it was not long before the new, and perhaps over-enthusiastic members had a real impact on the Society and Bob Partridge was elected Chairman. The Society then changed its name; having the word 'amateur' in its title was appropriate in that members had a genuine love for the subject, but the word could be perceived as somewhat pejorative. The new name was 'Manchester Ancient Egypt Society', the name it retains today.

Nowadays the society's monthly meetings may be addressed by lecturers of international repute or, following the earlier tradition, by members of the society, many of whom have become well known on the lecture circuit. Some are even called upon by television companies. Those who have had such experiences are aware that they are at the mercy of the producers. Bob Partridge recalls being invited to comment on the newly found tomb, KV63, in the Valley of the Kings on BBC News 24. He says that lot of museum experts prefer not to talk for fear of being misrepresented. As an example, Bob was asked whether this could be the tomb of Nefertiti. His response was deliberately vague and he said that it 'could be her, *or anyone else* for that matter.' The next day the website said 'Bob Partridge says this mummy could be Nefertiti'. In fact it turned out that there were no bodies in the tomb at all.

Programme makers want their documentaries to be dramatic and this sometimes causes problems and Bob was once told that he must try to envisage talking to a nine year old, since the target audience needs everything to be the biggest and best to keep the drama going. Points have to be reiterated after each of many advertisement breaks to make things punchy. Another society member, Colin Reader, who is a geologist by profession who was bitten by the Egyptology bug, is also called in to offer his expertise on TV. He has contributed to several programmes on the Sphinx.

In Greater Manchester there has been a long-standing tradition of education for interested adults dating right back to the early nineteenth century when philanthropic gentlemen set up mechanics institutes and other similar establishments to allow ordinary people access to some degree of education. Some of the Manchester Society's members such as Victor Blunden and Michael Tunnicliffe are involved in presenting courses on Egyptology for the WEA, independent study centres such as the Wilmslow Guild, and weekend courses at centres from Staffordshire to Cumbria.

Another major contribution from Manchester people to Egyptology has been the setting up of 'Ancient Egypt' magazine. The first editor, Miriam Bibby was also a product of the Manchester University certificate. When the publishers needed to find a new editor at short notice, they approached Bob Partridge, who was known to them through the MAES. Bob agreed on condition that Peter Phillips came too. They had already worked together on several books and had travelled to Egypt together. The partnership has been a great success. As they are both retired, they can (and do) spend most of their time on the production and promotion of the magazine which now has a readership around the world of around five thousand.

Each issue contains a wide variety of articles, all connected with some aspect of Egyptology. Many of them bring the reader right up to date with what is happening. Recently, for example, the magazine reported on the results of the DNA research into the family of Tutankhamun , only recently available. A regular feature is the fascinating collection of up-to-date news on what is currently happening in Egypt sent by the Egyptian correspondent, Ayman Wahby Taher of the University of Mansura. His feature ensures that the reader will be well-prepared next time he or she is in Egypt. Interestingly a number of articles have been written by Egyptologistswho are working and living and living in Manchester and the North West where much research is being undertaken. The magazine is full of well-presented and interesting material and should surely be prescribed reading for any Egyptomaniac. One of its projects is to adopt an Egyptological cause each year. The Friends of Nekhen and the Dahkleh Oasis Project, the Friends of the Petrie Museum and the Amarna Trust have all been beneficiaries.

The magazine has done a lot for Egyptology and promotes the activities of societies up and down the country. As Victor Blunden and Bob Partridge got involved in doing lectures round the country they became known by other societies and several people approached them to ask how to start. The magazine and the MAES have both been instrumental in helping with the formation of local societies. Now there are societies all round Greater Manchester perhaps because people are unwilling to come into the city. There are active groups in Tameside, North Manchester, Poynton, Wigan and Bolton, as well as some a little further away in places like the Wirral and Staffordshire.

The Horus Society based in Wigan is typical of these. It had its origins in an evening class taught by an enthusiast, John Johnson, who had just completed Rosalie David's certificate course. The class soon expanded its scope to develop a wide range of activity which included visits to Egypt and attendance at weekend Egyptological conferences. It was after one of these, in 2000, that it was decided to set up a properly constituted society which has proved to be very successful. It now has around one hundred and twenty members and holds six meetings a year. It can attract eminent speakers and is even, in June 2010, due to run a study day in collaboration with the Friends of the Petrie Museum thus establishing itself on the national Egyptological scene.

The Manchester Ancient Egypt Society puts on an exciting annual programme of monthly lectures, many by high-profile professional Egyptologists. Speakers over the last couple of years have included George Hart, Aidan Dodgson, Yvonne Harpur and David Rohl. A particular coup was to persuade Lord and Lady Carnarvon to come in April 2010 to talk about the Earl's great grandfather, the Fifth Earl, whose collaboration with Howard Carter is one of the most famous in the history of Egyptology. As a follow-up to this, a visit to Highclere Castle for society members was combined with access to the Griffith Institute to see the Tutankhamen Archive and a view of the newly refurbished Ashmolean Museum in Oxford.

The society also organises study days. A recent one was on the subject of Amenhotep III delivered by Joyce Tyldesley, Victor Blunden and Bob Partridge. Days like this and those organised by other societies and the KNH are trying to bridge the gap left by the withdrawal of classes which used to be held in the Department for Continuing Education. These had a devoted following which found itself adrift. Many of these people have transferred their allegiance to the new opportunities presented by these day schools and by the evening course sponsored by MAES taught by Victor Blunden.

These enthusiasts are the latest in a long tradition. They are following in the footsteps of many generations, back to the days of the noted Egyptologists. Petrie himself could expect an audience of hundreds when he came, as he did at least every year, to lecture in Manchester.[1]

---

[1] Most of the information in this section comes from interviews with a variety of people.

Fig 67 MAES members visiting Lord and Lady Carnarvon's home, Highclere Castle 2010

22. Enthusiasts and inspirations

Manchester is fortunate in its Egyptological resources, the Museum collection, the research facilities and the educational opportunities which it offers to the community at large. All this, deriving from the long-standing traditions with their roots in the nineteenth century, has produced a generation of people whose background was not originally in Egyptology as an academic study, but who have become enthusiasts and, eventually, professionals, passing their enthusiasm on to new generations. It would be impossible to write about all those who are, or have been, very active in Egyptology in Manchester, but the point can be proved by looking at the experiences of a selection of those most involved.

One of those who came through the extra-mural route, initially attending lectures in his home town and who went on to make a major contribution to the study of Egyptology in Manchester was Dr George Fildes, a retired GP from Bolton. He became one of the earliest participants in the certificate course. Like so many others he came into Rosalie David's orbit through a class which he attended. He began by going to WEA classes and became interested initially in Roman archaeology because of an extraordinarily enthusiastic lecturer who took his students on trips, one of which was to Hadrian's Wall. George was a favourite in his class, being an enthusiast himself, and was often asked to contribute to lectures. One member of the class was a Latvian lady who discovered Rosalie David's WEA classes and persuaded her to come and repeat the course in Bolton. George Fildes remembers that the audience was typical of such classes and included, two elderly ladies who were invariably late, sat in front row and promptly fell asleep. This was not George's style however and he took up the study of Egyptology with enthusiasm.

At that time Rosalie was asking for volunteers to help with the catalogue system in the Egyptology Department of the Museum. George took up the challenge with alacrity and it was the start of a close involvement on his part. There were three separate cataloguing systems running then, even one which dated from Margaret Murray's days before the First World War. At that time, in the late 1970s, the intention was to make paper lists and then to transfer them onto a computer, but this was before the development of the desktop model and required the use of the big mainframe computer at the University. Although this was not far from the Museum, there was a system of priorities and great demand for time on the computer which by today's standards was incredibly slow. It was only possible to work on the computer for the very short time allowed, then a message would appear, 'computer is closing down in fifteen minutes'. Under such constraints it took three and a half years just to catalogue the pottery. George was also given the job of sorting out the slate palettes, as well as working on some jewellery. One of his main contributions was the compilation of a history of the Museum which was never published but which is still used as a reference work in the Museum itself. The information which George Fildes assembled is fascinating and it records the involvement of a number of eminent individuals who might not be immediately associated with Egyptology. For example he discovered that when the Natural History Society was wound up in 1868, a committee was formed, the chair of which was Dr Joule, the physicist.

A visit to George Fildes' house reveals the extent of his enthusiasm. His study walls are lined with shelves containing hundreds of books, almost all of them on Egyptological topics and there is a small but interesting collection of genuine and replica shabti figures on display. In fact George donated a shabti from Seti I's tomb to the Museum. He had obtained this from a patient of his, who had been an assistant to Petrie in his youth, who had become later in life an avid collector of everything. When he died he left some items to George including a wooden shabti from which all the paint had gone. Now well into his nineties, the years have passed and George can no longer get into Manchester but his enthusiasm is undiminished.[1]

George Fildes' contribution has not been as visible as that of several individuals who have become full-time Egyptologists in some form or other. One, who came from a completely non-academic background but who has made a significant contribution to the propagation of Egyptology through his lectures for the WEA, Wilmslow Guild, and the now sadly defunct Extramural Department of the University, is Victor Blunden. He grew up in the 1960s in Greenheys, just across the road from the University, but in an era when the perception was that Higher Education was only for rich or brainy people. His inner city school did nothing to encourage boys with any academic aspirations so when he left he went straight to work in the civil service. When his parents became infirm, he shared their care with his sister. He went to work at the Post Office where he could do shift work which was more suitable to the situation. After his parents died, he and his sister looked round for new opportunities. She took up the piano while he decided to travel. His interest in astronomy led him to try to observe Halley's Comet on its rare visit in 1986. One of the places to see it was Egypt so he decided to go there as he could take in the pyramids at the same time. He picked the best tour he could find and cruised the full six hundred miles down the Nile from Aswan to Cairo. He had never been abroad before and was so bowled over by the temples and

---

[1] Fildes, George, 2006

Fig. 68 Victor Blunden

the art work, that he completely lost track of the comet. The trip was to change his life. Before he travelled he had decided to get some background knowledge so he joined a course which was being run in Manchester for people unable to get on the certificate course. It had been going for a year and he caught up in one term. From this he was encouraged to apply for the Certificate in Egyptology and had already been accepted before he went to Egypt. He did Rosalie David's course with all the people who later became important in MAES including Bob Partridge. Having done the course, he decided to apply to University. He gave up his job as a postman and was soon studying Ancient History and Archaeology at Manchester as a full-time mature student. Despite having to learn Latin in six months, helped by his sister for three hours a night, he worked on his essays at the weekends and found himself, much to his amazement, already in his thirties, 'in a class with all these brainy boys from prep and public schools.' He enjoyed his time in Manchester, did well in his degree and was offered a place at Liverpool to do an MA in Egyptology in 1993.

Having finished studying he was unemployed for four years, despite his qualifications. Pam Scott who lectured for the WEA asked him to stand in for her sometimes. He liked the work and, whilst working as a driving instructor, gradually increased his lectures through people ringing him and asking him to do more. When Pam's husband got a job in Geneva she left the area and a vacancy arose, which suited Victor. She recommended him to the WEA and the University and a new career developed. He says 'it was strange to be standing at the front of the lecture hall instead of sitting at the back' By this time he was Secretary of the MAES and had begun to think about forming a network of societies. He decided to produce a contact sheet so that

societies could swap their newsletters. He came up with the idea of a 'Directory' of British Egyptology Societies which included all sorts of information on more than thirty societies with a calendar of events and a location map for each of them. By 1999-2000 it was being more professionally produced. MAES started this and sent it to institutions like the British Museum, the Egyptian Embassy, and several Universities for their libraries. After four years it was suggested that other societies should produce the Directory, in rotation. The Sussex Society produced two good editions then passed the mantle to the Thames Valley Society but no further editions were produced. Since 2004 its publication has lapsed as the BES information is now provided on the Web instead, and its role has also been largely superseded by the Contacts/Events pages in the 'Ancient Egypt' magazine which publishes similar details. Victor still writes these pages and contributes regularly to the magazine on the subject of websites about ancient Egyptian topics. In the tradition set by Rosalie David of inspiring those who study with them, Victor has built up a large following of enthusiasts and has led many students back to Egypt on various study tours.[2]

The person who helped Victor to his first position in the academic teaching world was Pamela Scott, another notable product of Rosalie's certificate course. Many of those who have attended her classes on hieroglyphs speak highly of her ability and her knowledge, yet she too was not originally an Egyptologist, although her first degree in 1972 was in an associated discipline, Biblical Studies. This included studying Hebrew, Classical Greek, Archaeology and Comparative Religion. It was the last two that she found most interesting. So after university she followed a certificate course in archaeology and then joined Rosalie's extramural courses on Egyptian civilisation. In the meantime she had also taken a Postgraduate Diploma in Librarianship at Manchester Polytechnic and, in 1979, a Postgraduate Certificate in Education. In 1993 she took Rosalie David's Certificate in Egyptology, followed by an MPhil degree researching Graeco-Roman mummy portraits with special reference to the Manchester Museum collection. She says that she cannot remember a time when she was not interested in ancient history, but an early memory she has is of being fascinated by a serial in 'Look and Learn' magazine, about the adventures of a princess being taken by boat to the Egyptian court. After leaving university, she always attended some evening class or other, and in 1987 joined the Prestwich Egyptology group. Her daughter was about two at the time and she wanted something to keep her brain active. Her current expertise in hieroglyphics was from 'an amazing man called Jim Nuttall, a founding member of the Manchester Ancient Egypt Society. Since retiring from his job Jim had set about teaching himself hieroglyphs, mostly from Gardiner. A small group of us persuaded him to give us weekly classes, in someone's home. These continued for a few years, and gave me a good grounding in some of the basics of the grammar. Jim had a very analytical mind and was endlessly

[2] Blunden, Victor, 2006

patient with us poor duffers.' Later she attended Rosalie's extra-mural hieroglyphs classes, studying Egyptian texts. Her occasional courses, now sponsored by the Manchester Ancient Egypt Society are eagerly awaited.[3]

One of the most energetic and creative holders of the Certificate in Egyptology is Robert Partridge. He is a Trustee of the Egypt Exploration Society, Chairman of the Manchester Ancient Egypt Society, Editor of 'Ancient Egypt' magazine, which has an international reputation, and runs the Ancient Egypt Picture Library. He has run courses on Ancient Egypt, gives lectures in the UK and abroad and has made many TV appearances. He has also organized group trips to Egypt for the Manchester Ancient Egypt Society as well as being the 'expert' guide on tours for a specialist travel company. He had no background in Egyptology.

His first interest was sparked as a boy in Brixham when a small round plate inlaid with silver and copper was found buried in the garden. How it had come to be there was a mystery but it was Egyptian, albeit modern, probably a souvenir brought by a returning soldier from the First or Second World War. This prompted an inspection of a little-used set of encyclopaedia for all references to Egypt. Not long after, there was an article in his mother's woman's magazine about a trip to Egypt. That fired his enthusiasm, which was not dampened when the whole of ancient Egyptian history was dealt with at Grammar School in just one lesson. His interest led him to acquire books, starting with a copy of Christianne Desroches-Noblecourt's 'Tutankhamen' for Christmas. A book on what was perceived to be a 'boring' subject was considered an odd Christmas present for a ten year old and it cost the huge sum of three guineas. Bob joined the EES in 1968 but was not really able to pursue his interest until he came to Manchester. There were no local Egyptology societies, few, if any, documentaries on TV and only a few objects in museums. On a first visit to London in 1968 the British Museum did not feature on the list of sights his family wanted to see.

Bob worked for Barclays Bank in the West Country and was moved to Knutsford for a three year attachment in 1984. He was able to develop his interest by joining the Certificate Course and when it became clear that he was to remain in Manchester, he rapidly became heavily involved in local activities. This increased after he took early retirement.

The Certificate Course final dissertation (for which he received a Distinction) became the subject of his first book on an Egyptian topic, 'Faces of Pharaohs: Royal Mummies and Coffins from Ancient Thebes'. This was followed by 'Transport in Ancient Egypt' and 'Fighting Pharaohs: Weapons and Warfare in Ancient Egypt'. In addition Bob has written articles for several Egyptological and archaeological magazines as well of course for 'Ancient Egypt' Magazine. His most recent work has been

[3] Scott, Pamela 2007

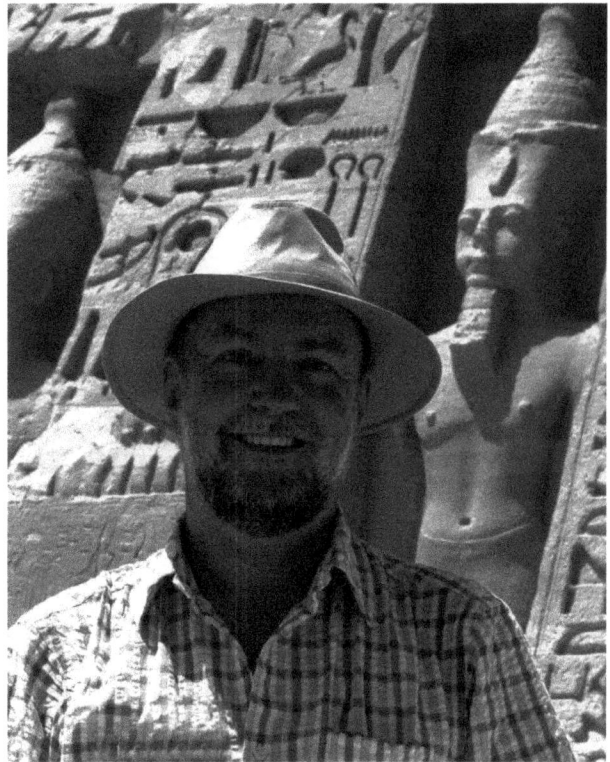

Fig.69 Bob Partridge, Editor of 'Ancient Egypt'

a chapter on transport in ancient Egypt in the two-volume 'Blackwell's Companion to Ancient Egypt' where Bob is one of many contributors.

Whilst on the Certificate Course Bob produced a regular newsletter for the course members, which was continued by others on subsequent courses. Before the publication of any Egyptology magazines and in a pre-internet age it was a good way of finding out what was happening in the world of Egyptology.

Besides his active involvement in both the local society and his editorship of the magazine, he has a photo library of about 30,000 slides and photos taken over thirty years of visiting Egypt (and over fifty individual trips). The picture library which is all catalogued and organised, now provides a resource for major publishers and researchers. A new application of his pictures has come through television where his images have been used in many programmes. Discovery Channel wanted to show a virtual tomb, preferably intact, with a painted chapel, goods and a burial chamber. No such tomb exists so they used his pictures to create a very believable burial chamber using the paintings from the tomb of Sennedjem and a selection of images of contemporary tomb goods now in various museums.

Bob's role as Editor of 'Ancient Egypt' magazine has provided many interesting opportunities and contacts in Egypt and around the world. Bob has met the Head of the Egyptian Supreme Council for Antiquities, Dr Zahi Hawass in Egypt and also at the opening of the Tutankhamun Exhibition at the O2 in London. This was a prestigious

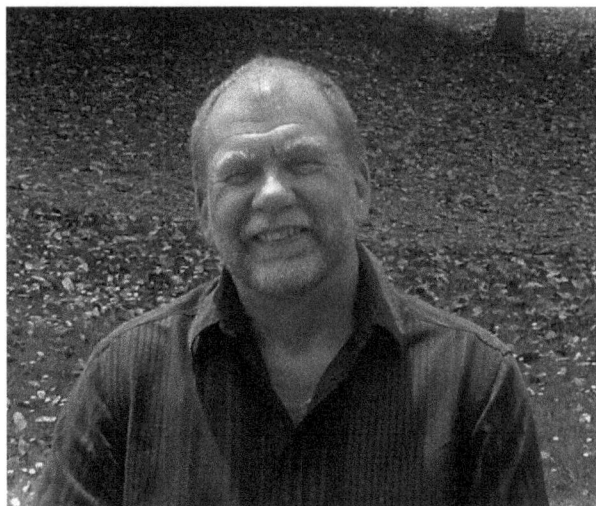

Fig. 70 Peter Phillips

occasion attended by Lord and Lady Carnarvon as well as MAES' own Audrey Carter, a relative of Howard.[4]

Bob's close colleague on the magazine is his Deputy Editor, Peter Phillips who is another example of someone who came into Egyptology from an unusual angle. He was an I.T. Manager in the University of Manchester and head of the internal databases, before taking early retirement. He had always been interested in Archaeology in a superficial way but has a lifelong interest in architecture. That seems to be in the blood because his great grandfather always wanted to be an architect but never made it, because he died too young to get training, having come from a farming background. He died in the 'flu epidemic after the First World War.

Peter was always fascinated by ancient ruins and took every chance to visit castles or other old buildings. When he met Bob Partridge and they talked about ruins in Egypt, his interest in this subject was sparked. The hypostyle hall at Karnak with its huge columns was what he really wanted to see. After that it was the Step Pyramid and how it evolved. This led on to a fascination with all things Egyptian and he too joined the Certificate in Egyptology course in Manchester.

When it came to the final dissertation, the most important part of the course, Peter chose to study ancient Egyptian columns. This was a topic which nobody had ever really looked at before; very little had been written on this subject, so his work involved much original research. He wrote his Dissertation (also receiving a Distinction) and thought little more of the subject until he met Rosalind Janssen who was giving a lecture at Poynton Egypt Group. She was the external examiner for the Certificate Course and she told Peter that his dissertation was really good and that he ought to publish it. This inspired him, with Bob Partridge's encouragement, to expand the work and publish the work as a book. They went to Egypt several times and studied and photographed probably every column. It was

only when they catalogued the photos that patterns began to emerge and it was possible to trace developments. The book, 'The Columns of Egypt' was published under their own auspices (along with Bob's book on Egyptian warfare) through their 'Peartree Publishing' brand. Peter is involved heavily in Egyptology, giving lectures all over the country and working on the magazine. He is also the Treasurer of MAES.[5]

Another active member of the MAES committee, not in this case a Mancunian but a proud 'Scouser', is Colin Reader. About ten years ago he was working as a geologist, looking at contamination of land by industrialisation. In his spare time he began reading some books by authors who were trying to develop an alternative history of Egypt. This stimulated his interest in Egyptology. One of the questions which kept coming up was the age of the Sphinx, with some scholars speculating that it was much older than had originally been thought. This theory was based on the weathering and the condition of the rocks. Colin began to question the ideas of these authors as their answer was so dramatically opposed to the traditional, so he began to research it from home as a hobby. He found that, surprisingly for such a well-known archaeological site, little information exists and any maps which do exist are poor and hard to get hold of. The best available source relating to groundwater level dates from 1830. Though this would seem at face value to be very dated information, in fact it is more relevant because it comes from before the Aswan Dam was built, and so in relation to the Sphinx it is more accurate. At the time it was just a hobby but Colin decided to go for a weekend to Cairo and this included a visit to Giza. He recalls, 'as soon as I got there I saw something I hadn't seen in any of the papers on the subject - which was that the Sphinx lies at the bottom of a hill, so when there was rainfall it would go downhill and the Sphinx at the bottom would catch all of it. I looked at the distribution of the erosion. People claimed to have mentioned it but no-one really explained it. I had a few more days in Cairo and really enjoyed myself. On the last day I went back to Giza and what I saw convinced me that it was built by Khafre and the erosion is run-off from rainfall, we know about flash floods in the Valley of the Kings and I'm convinced this is similar.'

He needed pictures but never had exactly the right one, so he contacted the EES who put him in touch with Bob Partridge. 'I phoned him up and he asked me over. I was very reticent at first, being an amateur in the face of an experienced Egyptologist but he said he had a good map (out of Barry Kemp's Egypt book) and it showed quarries. It was the first drawing I'd seen of the quarries used for building the pyramids. There's a massive quarry right behind the Sphinx which was used by Khufu and it put the Sphinx much earlier than Khufu.'

As he continued his research and read more he became more involved. Then the BBC, which was doing a programme

---

[4] Bob Partridge

[5] Peter Phillips

on the Sphinx, contacted him to make a contribution, having been given his name by Bob Partridge. He was asked if there was anything which could indicate evidence about the Sphinx. Colin pointed out a cut along the north side which Mark Lehner dates to the IVth Dynasty, near the Seti II temple. He predicted, correctly, that this cut would be a fresh cut and that the bit beyond it would be highly weathered. This started him on a new course which involved writing to people to discuss his theories. Amongst others, he wrote to Ian Matheson who has done work at Sakkara and the structures thought to be IInd Dynasty. Matheson replied that he could do with another geologist on his site. Colin says, 'I took a split second to decide and obviously accepted. So I fell into the role of geologist on the Sakkara survey project and I've done geological mapping at Sakkara. Ian's concession overlaps slightly with the Czech concession at Abu Sir so I got to work with them as well and I've done some TV work.' Every time one opportunity comes to an end something new turns up for him. Having had no knowledge of the ancient Egyptians to begin with he is now a great fan but he does not believe that they had fabulous technology. Instead they had intuition and manpower and they were tenacious in finding solutions. A visit to Aswan provoked a new train of thought. He is working on the idea that some vertical holes drilled into the rock were actually bore holes to check out the quality of the rock before they started to cut.

His joining the lecture circuit has provided new experiences. At a lecture at Cardiff in 1999 he met a geologist from the Department of Archaeology and Egyptology in Oxford who offered to print his work in 'Archaeometry' published by Oxford University. Another paper was published in David Rohl's New Chronology Forum. He has also been involved in Palarch, a Dutch forum on the internet.

He is proud of being quoted in a review of a book on the Sphinx, written by a French author. The reviewer commented that it was a pity the author had not quoted the debate on the dating of the Sphinx and in particular the work of the more sober views like those of Colin Reader. He is also amused by an article which appeared in the BBC Focus Magazine. It was a question and answer special with a line-up of experts, Patrick Moore, David Attenborough and Colin himself.

Colin's latest theories concern the use of mud to create the funerary causeways to the pyramids of Sakkara in the IVth Dynasty. Realising that there are Dynasty II tombs located round the head of the Abu Sir wadi he began to think about the environmental change at the end of the Old Kingdom which Karl Butzer, the great ecologist, had identified. At the head of the wadi, a green patch marks the remains of a lake. The greener wadi would be an extension of the Black Land where the Egyptians would feel safe, so they could put their tombs next to it and could safely walk through the Black Land without touching the area of chaos, the Red Land or desert. So Colin made a mental leap of faith and suggested that the mud causeways were an extension of the safe Black Land. He offered his thoughts to the JEA and

to his amazement they took his article and published it in full. He discovered that people thought it a very important paper. He has lectured in Reading on the geology of Egypt alongside professionals like Kent Weeks and Michael Wood. [6]

When talking to a variety of those who have studied or been actively involved in Egyptology locally, one name crops up regularly, that of Tony Taylor. He is regarded by those whose paths have crossed his, as the fount of all knowledge on all people working in Egyptology in Egypt itself. He is said to know everyone who is anyone and can put researchers in touch with the most useful person. If one needs access to a certain set of inscriptions, for example, Tony probably knows the man who can help.

He has had an interesting journey to arrive at this position. After a spell in the Royal Marines, he began his civilian professional life as a social worker and reached the position of Senior Advisor for Social Welfare to the Director of Social Services in Liverpool. He was involved in such important areas as the organisation of old people's homes, home helps and psycho-geriatric services. All this was a long way from Egyptology in which he only became involved when he took very early retirement at the age of 45. He decided to take up something in which he could really get interested so, remembering an early fascination with the stories of Moses and Joseph which he had heard in Sunday School as a child, he began to think about following their journeys. Whilst in the Marines he had spent time in the desert and liked the desert way of life. He was able to attend a series of lectures on Egyptology and through this made contact with Rosalie David who was 'way ahead in her thinking' and whose certificate course was the only one of its kind at the time. He had not come across her work before this but found the course, which he took up around 1992 very inspiring. It gripped him because he was learning what he wanted to learn. Since then Tony has spent a good deal of his time in Egypt. He was not only looking at ancient history, however, one of his priorities was to find out about the modern country. He lived with the Bedouin for a while and learnt their language. This gave him a tool with which to get closer to the Egyptian people and to make the many contacts which he now has. He is able to visit Egypt frequently and often takes the opportunity of staying with his adopted family in Sinai. Through these Bedouin friends he has established contacts with many interesting people including the local Bedouin doctor. He relishes being a part of this family and particularly enjoys the title of 'Uncle' which they have bestowed upon him. He believes that the experience he gained in his professional life has given him the ability to network for which he is well-known. [7]

Another well known local personality owes her celebrity to the fact that she is distantly related to Howard Carter, the discoverer of Tutankhamun. Audrey Carter first became interested in Egypt in her childhood through reading her

---

[6] Reader, Colin 2007
[7] Taylor, Tony 2008

*Fig. 71 Audrey Carter at the
Pharmacy and Medicine Conference*

mother's set of mythology books full of old photos, some of which were of mummies. Her mother mentioned that Howard Carter was a relative but Audrey put it to the back of her mind, though she was always conscious of it. She took a trip to Egypt in 1964 and remembers little but knows she enjoyed it. Over the next few years her travels took her to other places like Greece. She became interested again in Egypt in 1984 when she had a temporary job with the Manchester University Press as secretary in the Science and Arts section. At the time Rosalie David was doing a book and she came in and Audrey met her. There was a competition amongst the staff to invent a title. The winner came up with 'Evidence Embalmed'.

Audrey joined the Certificate Course along with Bob Partridge and Victor Blunden in 1986. Howard Carter seemed to be the obvious choice for her to study for her dissertation. Her brother helped to work out the genealogy and found that Howard was the youngest of 11 children. He was rather sickly and brought up by maiden aunts. There are still relatives living in Suffolk. Thomas, her mother's father, was Howard's cousin.

This family connection has allowed Audrey to have some interesting experiences. There are still local people in Egypt who have not forgotten Howard Carter. The face of the guardian in the tomb of Tutankhamun lit up when Audrey was introduced as a relative of Carter. On another occasion in Cairo, her group stopped at a café and their leader introduced her to a middle-aged gentleman who was a descendant of the Al-Rasul brothers who were the notorious tomb robbers in the time of Petrie and Carter.

She was able to be present in Chelsea when a blue plaque was put up in memory of her relative. She went as an honoured guest to the O2 Stadium for the Gala evening at the start of the 2008 Tutankhamun Exhibition. She was able to listen to the press session and meet Prince Charles. Lord and Lady Carnarvon, whom she found a delightful couple, were next to her and she found that he is more interested in Egypt than his father, who had apparently believed in the curse of the tomb and was more interested in horse-racing in any case. The daughter of Evelyn Herbert, the fifth Earl's daughter was at the reception too. During the wine and canapés she met other interesting people and was impressed by Zahi Hawass, the Head of the Supreme Council of Antiquities whom she found to be very charismatic.

Her last job was with North West Arts. On retirement she decided to get a degree to keep her brain ticking. Her MPhil degree took three years of hard work with Rosalie David as her supervisor. Her thesis was on religious and social artefacts from Gurob in the XVIIIth Dynasty in Manchester Museum. She was working under some difficulty, since the decorators had painted over the locks of some display cases. She administered the certificate course temporarily and enjoyed the work but had to give up through ill-health. Most recently she attended the grand opening of the Carter House in Luxor which has just been restored and made into a museum.[8]

These are just a few of the enthusiasts who are involved in Egyptology in the Greater Manchester area. It would not be possible to cover every person involved. There are hard-working members of the MAES Committee such as Muriel O'Shea who acts as membership secretary and edits the society's newsletter, 'Djehuty' and Gillian Cook, for many years the organiser of a regular raffle which benefits Egyptian causes. She also organises society trips, including the 2010 visit to Oxford and Highclere Castle, the home of the Earl of Carnarvon..

At the Griffith Institute members were shown an item to which their raffle money had contributed. This was a sketchbook belonging to Amelia Edwards which has watercolour pictures and ink sketches of her trip up the Nile. The Griffith Institute staff are now able to conserve this in ideal conditions for posterity. There are many members of the society who travel to Egypt regularly, some more than once a year. Other society members have been and are engaged in their own research, some, like Tony Judd, already in print.

It is clear from all this that Egypt, both ancient and modern, exercises a spell. Once under its influence, people are unlikely to break free. The evidence for ancient Egypt seems to be vast, yet the more that can be learned, the more the huge gaps in our knowledge become evident. This means that there is still much to be done by this and successive generations of scholars and Egyptophiles.

---

[8] Carter, Audrey 2008

Fig. 72 The MAES Committee 2010. One member, Colin Reader is not pictured.

Fig.73 Colin Reader new Chairman of MAES 2011

23. A continuing tradition

The remarkable interest in Egyptology in Greater Manchester has had a long history. Its roots reach back into the nineteenth century when a number of factors combined to lay the foundations of the great collections of Egyptological material which still exist in the area. The story is not yet complete, as exciting new developments are emerging all the time.

The factors which came together in the nineteenth century combined to create the opportunities which later generations were able to take up. The huge wealth derived from the cotton industry and the character of some of those who made their fortunes from it was a major element in the building up of the great local collections. This might not have gone into Egyptology, however, without two further important driving forces; the close links which the textile towns built up with Egypt because of the cotton trade, particularly after the cotton famine caused by events in America, and the deeply felt religious views of many of the magnates involved, both contributed to the enormous interest in Egypt. The commercial links created not only wealth, but also a fascination with the ancient civilisation of the country which the cotton men were visiting regularly on business. Their religious fervour gave them an insatiable desire to prove the events recorded in the Bible, particularly those relating to the period of the Jewish sojourn in Egypt and the Exodus.

The prosperity of the cotton industry coincided with the period when exploration of Egyptian sites was at its height. W.M.F.Petrie's pioneering excavations were an inspiration to many other scholars and the possibilities for acquiring material to stock new museums as well as private collections seemed endless. The collections which were assembled in the towns around Manchester still stand as a reminder of these halcyon days. Sadly, cotton is no longer King in this area, the mills are long-gone and the fortunes no doubt are mainly dissipated. The legacy, however lives on. The foundations laid in the latter part of the nineteenth and early part of the twentieth century have provided support for the continuing tradition of Egyptological study and widespread enthusiasm.

Petrie's influence was far-reaching. He had a particular interest in Manchester and paid frequent visits, visiting friends, attending meetings of the Egyptian and Oriental Society and delivering lectures. An enthusiastic group of academics and local worthies grew up and Egyptology prospered in the area. The subject had tended to be rather theoretical in its early days but by the early twentieth century scholars had begun to take a more scientific approach. Some of their work was particularly focussed on textiles. Petrie had brought over large quantities of samples, many of which were complete garments. Naturally the local experts were fascinated by ancient fabrics, the way in which they were made and the dyestuffs which were used, hoping to glean ideas which could be transferred to the local industry.

The other major work in these early years was the study of human remains in a scientific manner. Frequently before this, mummies had been unrolled purely for the prurient interest they engendered. Audiences were fascinated by the spectacle and loved this macabre post-prandial entertainment. Manchester's first multi-disciplinary mummy study under the leadership of Margaret Murray was a totally different type of spectacle. The audience was carefully selected and only interested in the advancement of scientific knowledge.

In the years which followed there is much evidence of careful scholarship being applied to the various local collections. Detailed correspondence on scraps of hieroglyphic inscriptions and close study of objects are recorded in correspondence. Winifred Crompton, for example had an article published in the JEA relating to two small clay balls containing human hair from the Manchester collection.[1] Nowadays these might well have been subjected to close microscopic and other scientific tests but these were not available to Miss Crompton.

Despite two world wars and their consequent disruption, local interest in Egyptology continued into the mid-twentieth century. At this point it took a new and exciting turn. The setting up of the Manchester Mummy Project with its new protocols and its multi-disciplinary team set the standard for scholarship worldwide. The proximity of the Manchester Museum to the hospital helped to facilitate the study of human remains and other material. CAT and MRI scans can be easily arranged now that the KNH Centre is situated in the Stopford Building which is part of the Medical School. The department's reputation which has been built up since the 1970s has encouraged many researchers to make use of the expertise available. The mummy tissue bank is a resource which can be tapped by scholars from elsewhere. Every year the academic qualifications offered by the KNH Centre are achieved by new generations of students so that the now well-established tradition will be able to continue.

One of the major reasons for the development of Egyptology in the Manchester area has been the contribution made by a series of remarkable individuals. Without Jesse Haworth's generous contributions for example, there would never have been such a major collection of Egyptian material

---

[1] JEA Crompton, Winifred

Fig.74 Part of the new Mummy Tissue Bank storage

in the Manchester Museum. It is interesting to note that many of the major players in this area have been women. Apart from the wives of the benefactors who certainly gave enthusiastic support to their husbands, there were a number of others who worked tirelessly, following the example of Amelia Edwards whose work for the EEF was of huge importance. Kate Bradbury of Ashton under Lyne took personal responsibility for cleaning and cataloguing much of Petrie's material which became part of the collection. Annie Barlow in Bolton almost single-handedly built up support for Egyptian exploration. These two were from wealthy textile families. Perhaps even more notable was the contribution of Winifred Crompton, less well known and from a less moneyed, though well-educated background. Her thorough approach and devoted work ensured that the museum collection continued to be developed and studied.

The modern work on Egyptology in Manchester also owes its success to a remarkable woman. The Professor of Egyptology, Rosalie David has been the major constant in the work carried out in Manchester. She was the moving spirit in the setting up of the Mummy Project and has gone on through the next three decades to devise and carry out a series of major projects. Her enthusiasm and creative approach, together with her chain of contacts at home and abroad have opened up new areas for research. She has provided her teams of colleagues and successive generations of students, both those in full-time education and those in continuing education, with encouragement and inspiration.

One of Professor David's talents is to identify and develop the strengths of others. Her original multi-disciplinary team combined the expertise of people with a wide range

of backgrounds. She was also able to take advantage of the facilities for state of the art research which existed in the vicinity. The time was right for this kind of development and she had the backing of the University which was of paramount importance. The establishment over the years of a range of academic courses has provided a foundation for the ongoing work which will take the study of Egyptology well into the future.

It was the accepted belief at the time she took over that science and arts disciplines were two very separate studies. Egypt was still, to some degree, considered to have had an inferior civilisation to those of the Classical cultures. Most Egyptology was biased towards the arts, using language and material culture as its focus. Since the majority of the collections contained a high proportion of sculptures and paintings collected from tombs in an earlier era, this aesthetic approach is understandable. It was Manchester's new research into Mummy Studies and the academic courses resulting from it which allowed a more scientific emphasis. The MSc course, for example, offered by the KNH Centre is a rare example of a degree in Egyptology which is science, not arts, based. The great advantage of this course is that it allows those from both sides of the academic spectrum to participate. Through this course opportunities are available for the study of material using the most modern technological advances. This gives Egyptology a relevance to modern times which has not always been the case.

Now that the KNH Centre has its permanent base after a somewhat peripatetic few years, it is in a position to consolidate the work which has already been done. It has laboratory space which can accommodate a range of equipment as well as an experienced team contributing

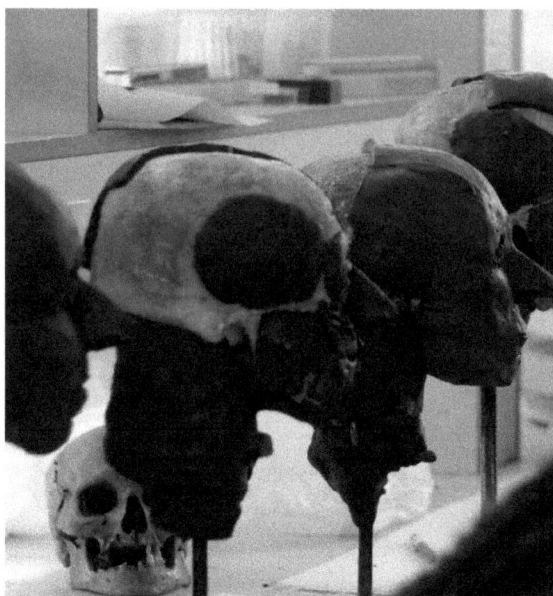

*Fig.75 Heads from a facial reconstruction workshop ready for
Professor David to inspect*

to both research and teaching. The mummy tissue bank is now properly established in the Centre housed in ideal storage conditions.

There are plans to hold regular Summer Schools; the first in June 2010 proved a great success. There will also be at least one Study Day each year and two in years when there is no Summer School. Short courses in Egyptology are now being offered on the internet, covering various aspects of the subject. Other exciting educational developments are also in the pipeline. Meanwhile the post graduate courses continue to train new generations in the techniques of bio-medical Egyptology.

New ideas are constantly emerging from the KNH Centre. A recent article in the 'Lancet' was the result of a chance conversation between Rosalie David and the cardiologist, Anthony Heagerty. Their discussion of the evidence of atherosclerosis in Egyptian mummies led them to speculate about the diet of the ancients. Evidence from the inscriptions at Abydos attests to offerings made in temple rituals containing large amounts of animal fats. As these offerings were later consumed by the priests, it seemed logical to suppose that there was a causal link between the diet and the disease found in their mummies. Amie Kershaw, a dietician, was given translations of the lists of offerings and was able to confirm the theory. This article was reported worldwide.[2]

Another area of interest has been the relative lack of evidence for cancer in the ancient population. An article in 'Cancer Nature' by Professor David and Professor Zimmerman, the Oncologist, looks at the arguments put forward to explain this. One suggestion has been that the relatively short lifespan of the Egyptians meant that cancers did not have time to develop. However there is evidence that other conditions, such as arthritis, normally associated

with ageing, did develop. In any case, there is no evidence of childhood cancers which are common today. Another possibility is that malignancies might not have survived in mummified tissue. Experiments on modern examples have proved that this is not the case. The evidence therefore points to a conclusion that modern problems are caused by lifestyle and environmental factors.[3]

On the research side, alongside the Elliot Smith project, funded by the Wellcome Trust, there are major projects afoot. One of these, studying animal mummies, is aimed at identifying evidence of zoonoses, diseases which can be transmitted between human and animal species. This could provide valuable information for researchers into modern disease patterns.

Another exciting development is the establishment of a link with the Bio-informatics Department in the University, which, together with Cambridge, is one of the world leaders in the field. New possibilities allow medical researchers to ask questions and the computer to generate further questions to be addressed. Current studies are aimed at assessing whether this can be applied to ancient Egyptian data, for example, from disease patterns and populations found in particular cemeteries.

Ideas feed on one another and generate further ideas. The field has endless possibilities and it is a challenge to decide which should have priority. It is certain however that the Bio-medical projects carried out in the KNH Centre have much to offer, not only in ancient studies but in modern medical research. The ancient Egyptians did not disappear, they are still there. A continuous population covering a period of 7000 years offers unique opportunities for genetic and epidemiological study, which could be of real importance in modern medical work.

---

[2] The Lancet 2010

[3] Cancer Nature 2010

Bibliography

Books and articles

Anonymous 1902 *The John Rylands Library*, Printed for private circulation

Archbold, Rick and David, Rosalie, 2000. *Conversations with Mummies* Harper Collins

Bowker, B, 1928 in Longworth , James H. *The Cotton Mills of Bolton*, Bolton, Bolton Museum and Art Gallery

David , Rosalie and Tapp, Eddie, (eds.)1984 *'Evidence Embalmed'* Manchester, Manchester University Press

David , Rosalie and Tapp, Eddie 1992 *The Mummy's Tale* London, Michael O'Mara Books

David , Rosalie 1980 *The Macclesfield Collection of Egyptian Antiquities* Warminster, Aris and Phillips

David, Rosalie1979, *Manchester Mummy Project* Manchester, Manchester University

David, R (ed) 1978 *Mysteries of the Mummies* London, Book Club Associates

David, Rosalie (ed) 2008 *Egyptian Mummies and Modern Science* , Cambridge University Press

Drower, Margaret 1995 *Flinders Petrie, a life in Archaeology* University of Wisconsin

Edwards, A.B, 1877 *A Thousand Miles Up the Nile* London: Longmans

Edwards, Amelia B. 1892 *Pharaohs, Fellahs and Explorers* London: James Osgood,Mc Ilwraine & co.

Gardiner, Alan,1927 *Egyptian Grammar* Oxford. Griffith Institute , Ashmolean Museum

Griffith, A.S, 1910 *Catalogue of the Egyptian Collection from Kahun and Gurob*. Manchester Museum

Manchester Faces and Places1897 Vol.IX *Edward Schunck* Manchester, J.G. Hammond & co

Manchester Faces and Places 1900 Vol XI pp35-41*John Rylands and Enriqueta Rylands* Manchester, J.G. Hammond & co

Mills ,William Haslam, 2000 *Grey Pastures*, The Chapels Society, London

Griffith, A. S. 1910 *The Manchester Museum Handbook, Catalogue of Egyptian Antiquities*, Manchester, Sherratt and Hughes

Heape, Charles and Heape, Richard 1904. *Records of the Family of Heape*. Printed for presentation to the family only.

Kanawati, Naguib et al.1993.*The Tombs of El- Hagarsa, vol.II* Australian Centre for Egyptology, Sydney

Kidd, Alan J. & Roberts K. W. (eds)1985. *City, class and culture* .Manchester: Manchester University Press

Longworth , James H. 1987.*The Cotton Mills of Bolton*, Bolton, Bolton Museum and Art Gallery

Murray, A. Margaret 1963. *My First Hundred Years*. London, W. Kimber

Petrie,W.M. Flinders Petrie,1931 *Seventy Years in Archaeology*, Sampson Low, Marston & Co. Ltd.: London

Rees, Joan,1998. *Amelia Edwards*. London: Rubicon press

Robinson, W. Gordon,1955 *Lancashire Congregational Union*, Manchester

Thomas, Angela *The Barefoot Aristocrats and the making of an Egyptian Collection*. In Thomas Schneider & Kasia Szpakowska (eds), Egyptian Stories. A British Egyptological tribute to Alan B. Lloyd on the Occasion of His Retirement. Alter Orient und Altes Testament Veroffentllichungen zur Kultur und Geschichte des Alten Orient und dea Alten Testament AOAT 347. Munster 2007, pp 417-436

Thomas, Angela *The Midgleys of Bolton and their Contribution to the Scientific Examination of Ancient textiles*: Archaeological Textiles Newsletter 45 Autumn 2007 pp21-25

Unwin, Richard 2008 *Riversvale Hall*, Failsworth Historical Society

Bibliography: Archive and unpublished sources

Petrie Museum Archive Correspondence:-
W.F.Petrie to A.B.Edwards and AB Edwards to W.F.Petrie
Jesse Haworth, to W.F.Petrie
Greville Chester to W.F.Petrie

Griffith Institute:-
Dodgson Correspondence
Journal of the visit of Kate Bradbury and Amelia Edwards to America

EES archive
Correspondence :A B Edwards to WF M Petrie
Journal in Amelia Edwards' own hand

Manchester Museum unpublished texts
Fildes, George, Manchester Museum: Owens College Report Summaries 1895-1985
Fildes, George, The history of the Manchester Museum

Manchester Museum Correspondence:-
Winifred Crompton with various correspondents
Mary Shaw with various correspondents

Bolton Museum and Archive:
Documents relating to the visit of King Fuad to Bolton, 1927
Heywood Diaries1843
Diaries of a visit to Egypt: Assman Granville 1905

Macclesfield Museum Archives
Marianne Brocklehurst's diary
Marianne Brocklehurst's sketch books

Bibliography: Lecture drafts
Berg, Harry,1990 Set- god or devil? Lecture to Manchester Amateur Ancient Egypt Society
Blunden, Victor 1990, Tombs of the New Kingdom at Thebes. lecture to Manchester Amateur Ancient Egypt Society
Campbell, Jacqueline, 2006. Nutrition in Ancient Egypt. Draft of lecture to National Research Centre, Cairo
Fildes,Alan c 1990 In the shadow of the pyramids, lecture to Manchester Amateur Ancient Egypt Society
Moon, Brenda, 2000 A fearful outbreak of Egyptology, lecture given to ASTENE in Manchester
Moxon, John, The Decline of Pyramid Building, lecture to Manchester Amateur Ancient Egypt Society

Websites

http://adbonline.anu.edu/biogs/A1106656
Blunt, Michael J. 1988, Sir Grafton Elliot Smith(1871-1937) Australian Dictionary of Biography vol. II, Melbourne University Press pp 645-646
http://www.chriscooksey.demon.co.uk/schunck/
Henry Edward Schunck
http://www.infed.org/settlements/manchester_art_museum_and_university_settlement
Eagles,Stuart   2009,Thomas Coglan Horsfall and Manchester Art Museum and University Settlement
http://www.thelancet.com/journals/lancet/article/PIIS0140-6736(10)60294-2/fulltext
A.Rosalie David,Amie Kershaw, Anthony Heagerty: Atherosclerosis and diet in ancient Egypt
http://www.boltonmuseums.org.uk/about/collections-overview/egyptology-overview
http://www.BoltonNews.newsprint.co.uk
http://www.brown.edu/Research/Breaking_Ground/bios/Davies/Nina
Strudwick, Nigel: Nina de Garis Davies

Bibliography : Interviews

Blunden, Victor, 2006
Campbell, Jacqueline 2007
Carter, Audrey2008
Cockitt, Jenefer 2010
Counsell, David 2009 by telephone
David, Rosalie 2005
Denton, John 2008
Drower, Margaret 2006
Fildes, George,2006
Finch, Jacqueline, 2007
Forshaw, Roger, 2009
Isherwood, Ian 2007
KNH, 2006
Lambert, Patricia Lambert-Zazulak 2005
Martin, Barbara, 2008

McCreesh, Natalie 2009
Metcalfe, Ryan 2010
Neave, Richard 2007
Partridge, Robert 2007
Phillips, Peter 2007
Reader, Colin 2007
Scott, Pamela 2007 by e-mail
Tapp, Edmund 2008
Taylor, Tony 2008
Thomas, Angela, 2007
Tyldesley, Joyce 2008

Index

www.ingramcontent.com/pod-product-compliance
Lightning Source LLC
Chambersburg PA
CBHW061008030426
42334CB00033B/3410